Oil, Money,
and the Mexican Economy

Westview Replica Editions

The concept of Westview Replica Editions is a response to the continuing crisis in academic and informational publishing. Library budgets for books have been severely curtailed. Ever larger portions of general library budgets are being diverted from the purchase of books and used for data banks, computers, micromedia, and other methods of information retrieval. Interlibrary loan structures further reduce the edition sizes required to satisfy the needs of the scholarly community. Economic pressures (particularly inflation and high interest rates) on the university presses and the few private scholarly publishing companies have severely limited the capacity of the industry to properly serve the academic and research communities. As a result, many manuscripts dealing with important subjects, often representing the highest level of scholarship, are no longer economically viable publishing projects--or, if accepted for publication, are typically subject to lead times ranging from one to three years.

Westview Replica Editions are our practical solution to the problem. We accept a manuscript in camera-ready form, typed according to our specifications, and move it immediately into the production process. As always, the selection criteria include the importance of the subject, the work's contribution to scholarship, and its insight, originality of thought, and excellence of exposition. The responsiblity for editing and proofreading lies with the author or sponsoring institution. We prepare chapter headings and display pages, file for copyright, and obtain Library of Congress Cataloging in Publication Data. A detailed manual contains simple instructions for preparing the final typescript, and our editorial staff is always available to answer questions.

The end result is a book printed on acid-free paper and bound in sturdy library-quality soft covers. We manufacture these books ourselves using equipment that does not require a lengthy make-ready process and that allows us to publish first editions of 300 to 600 copies and to reprint even smaller quantities as needed. Thus, we can produce Replica Editions quickly and can keep even very specialized books in print as long as there is a demand for them.

About the Book and Author

Oil, Money, and the Mexican Economy: A Macroeconometric Analysis
Francisco Carrada-Bravo

In the mid-1970s, unemployment, inflation, and monetary disturbances were dominant forces in the Mexican economy. Beginning in late 1977, however, the situation drastically changed. The discovery of enormous oil fields, combined with structural and social factors, vastly improved the nation's prospects, and in terms of business cycles, its economy moved from trough to peak.

In assessing these changes, Dr. Carrada constructs a macroeconometric model--based on the monetary approach to the balance of payments--to deal in the short-run with structural features of Mexico's economy. He then applies his model to a variety of scenarios in order to explore the short-run dynamic impact of oil revenues on real incomes, private and government expenditures, private and public investment, prices, inflation, money supply, and balance of payments. Incorporating theoretical and empirical evidence of how expectations affect levels of economic activity and inflation, Dr. Carrada's model is applicable also to the conditions of other oil-rich developing countries.

Dr. Carrada is director of economic studies and associate professor of economics at the Monterrey Institute of Technology in Mexico.

Oil, Money, and the Mexican Economy: A Macroeconometric Analysis

Francisco Carrada-Bravo

Westview Press / Boulder, Colorado

A Westview Replica Edition

Copyright © 1982 by Westview Press, Inc.

Published in 1982 in the United States of America by
    Westview Press, Inc.
    5500 Central Avenue
    Boulder, Colorado 80301
    Frederick A. Praeger, President and Publisher

Library of Congress Catalog Card Number: 82-50687
ISBN: 0-86531-902-2

Printed and bound in the United States of America

TO MY PARENTS

TEODORO

AND

MARIA DEL CARMEN CARRADA

Contents

Tables and Figures

Acknowledgements

This study, of which my doctoral dissertation is an earlier version, was possible thanks to the help of many individuals and institutions. Among the persons who deserve special mention are Professor Barry W. Poulson, chairman of my dissertation committee, who reviewed at length the manuscript and suggested changes that improved both the content and the style of the study; Professor Malcom Dowling from whose vast econometric and macroeconomic knowledge in developed and developing countries this work has greatly benefited; Professor Jacob K. Atta who gave me very valuable advice in critical periods of the research work. To all of them my gratitude.

To my wife Lilia who over the years, and especially the years of graduate school, provided me with support, companionship and strength; our daughters Lilia del Carmen and Maria Elena who helped many times to dispel the black moods of an author whose work often failed to be "in progress."

I am also indebted to my sponsors: the National Council of Science and Technology of Mexico (CONACYT), the administration of the Lincoln-Juarez Scholarship, the International Studies Center of the University of Colorado, and the Instituto Tecnologico y de Estudios Superiores de Monterrey (ITESM), who provided the required funding and all available facilities to make this work in the United States possible.

Finally, I would like to thank Enedina Sanchez-Gutierrez who bore the drudgery of typing and Lourdes Olvera for her artwork.

The responsiblity for what follows rests with the author.

1
Mexico:
A Structural Analysis

THE GEOGRAPHY OF MEXICO

Mexico is located in the American Continent within the Northern Hemisphere in the latitude where most desert regions are located. Water supply is a perpetual problem inland, since no large river crosses it.

Area

Mexico covers a total of 761,000 square miles[1] (1,958,201 square kilometers) which places Mexico as the thirteenth largest country in the world. It is bordered by the Gulf of Mexico to the east, the Pacific Ocean to the west, the United States to the north, Belize and Guatemala to the south.

Climate

Mexico is cut by the tropic of cancer which divides the country into two general weather systems. Northern Mexico is subject to wildly fluctuating temperatures during the year. The southern parts are tropical, and the temperatures within the remaining corridor are moderate.

Half of Mexico is very dry, receiving less than 24 inches of rainfall annually. This half is mostly the northern plateau regions, where rain falls on the seaward slopes, and evaporates rapidy on the high inland plateaus. The Baja California Peninsula receives the least precipitation of all areas, only 2 to 4 inches

---

[1] Mexico City Chamber of Commerce, Mexico 1980, Compendium of Mexican Data and Statistics, Mexico, Sept. 1980, p. 15.

per year. By contrast, in the southern seaward slopes
of the Sierra Madre Oriental of the Tuxtlas Region rainfall exceeds 100 inches per year.

Topography

Mexico has a variety of topological features. The
Baja peninsula runs for approximately 760 miles parallel
to the Mexican mainland separated from it by the Gulf of
California. It varies in width from 25 to 150 miles.
The northern part of Mexico stretches along a 1,300 mile
border with the United States.
Mountain ranges, the Sierra Madre Occidental and the
Sierra Madre Oriental, line two large plains, the Northern Plateau and the Mexican Plateau, running from the
south to the north of Mexico City. To the southeast of
Mexico is the Transversal Volcanic Mountain Range. In
this range are Mexico's highest peaks - Orizaba (18,700
m^2) and Popocatepetl (17,883 m^2). To the southwest is
the New Volcanic Mountain Range which creates much of
the flow of the Balsas River. But on the south side of
the Balsas River is the Sierra Madre del Sur Range running along the southern coast and rising from the mouth
of the Balsas River at the northwest end to the Gulf of
Tehuantepec at the southwest end. The shape of the
country resembles a horn of plenty with the Yucatan as
the small end of the horn. The northward thrust of the
Yucatan into the Gulf of Mexico forms the eastern shore
of the Bay of Campeche. The Yucatan Peninsula is general
ly flat to rolling and composed of porous and soluble
limestone. Drainage seeps through the limestone carving
out caves and producing sinks from sunken caverns.
In the anterior, water supply is a problem. No large
rivers transverse the interior plains. Evaporation is
rapid. Rain falling on the two Sierra Madre mountain
ranges flows either to the Pacific or to the Gulf of Mexi
co. The water flowing to the plains largely evaporates.
The rivers Grijalva-Usumacinta and Papaloapan account for
about 40 percent of the total flow of Mexico's river.
These are in the southern portion of Mexico.

SOCIAL AND POLITICAL FRAMEWORK

Historical Perspective

In the year 1521[2] Mexico became a territory of Spain
and remained as such for almost three centuries. The
colony was named by the spaniard rulers as "The New

---

[2]Fry Bartolome de las Casas, Brevísima Relación de la Destrucción
de las Indias, Colección Metropolitana, México, September 1974,
Departamento del Distrito Federal, p. 38.

Spain" and included most of Mexico's current boundaries plus the states of Texas, California, Arizona, New Mexico and part of Colorado. In 1810 an independence war led by the catholic priest Miguel Hidalgo broke out. After a decade of warfare the spaniard rule was over, and the country gained political autonomy. Independence was followed by a long transition period which was brought under control by Gral. Porfirio Diaz who ruled the country for 30 years. In 1910 Gral. Diaz was toppled and expelled from the country in what seemed to be a bloodless political transition. However, the murder of Mr. Francisco Madero, successor of Gral. Diaz, prompted a wave of violence that provided the grounds for the emergence of a handful of "caudillos" who were the founding fathers of the political party which under different names has been in Mexican politics the ruling force since 1929.

Political Framework

The ruling party took roots in 1929 as the Partido Nacional Revolucionario and was formed by the coalition of many contending factions. In 1935 it was renamed "Partido de la Revolucion". This party encompassed several broad functional interest groups by admitting members from these factions, namely peasants, laborers, the military and the "popular" and middle class sections to the party executive committee. Today the party is named "Partido Revolucionario Institucional". It defies efforts to pigeonhole the system as a democracy, dictatorship or other clean-cut category.

This characteristic derives from Mexico's unique method of political succession. The PRI, before the termination of the 6-year presidential term office, picks the successor to the incumbent. Since the PRI has not encountered significant political opposition, for the past 50 years the hand-picked candidate has almost virtual assurance of election. This lack of viable opposition is vividly shown in the current election where budget and planning Minister Miguel de la Madrid Hurtado is expected to carry more than 90 percent of the popular vote against other endorsed presidential oponents.

Organization of the Mexican Government. The newly elected President has under current laws the right to appoint all cabinet members among which are the following:

Secretary of Interior
Secretary of Foreign Affairs
Secretary of Defense
Secretary of Navy
Secretary of the Treasury

and Public Credit
Secretary of Government Properties and
Industrial Development
Secretary of Commerce
Secretary of Agriculture and Water
Resources
Secretary of Communications and
Transportation
Secretary of Human Settlement and
Public Workers
Secretary of Public Education
Secretary of Health and Welfare
Secretary of Labor and Social Welfare
Secretary of Agrarian Reform
Secretary of Tourism
Attorney General
Director of the National Oil Company

The turnover in cabinet posts at election time is
quite large since almost no one is allowed to hold the
same post for more than one term of six consecutive years
years.

Diagram 1, depicts the organization of the Mexican
Government. (The relationship of the President and the
rest of the government body is shown).

The Mexican Constitution. The present constitution
was adopted in 1917. There are several aspects of the
constitution which are noteworthy. The constitution is
frequently amended but the strength of the presidency
over all branches of government remains unaltered. In
fact, the Congress has no power to override a presidential veto. Some have called this institution of
power "the six year of democratic dictatorship". Provision is made for the "collective" ownership of
land, waters, seas, natural resources and sources of
power and fuel." The right of amparo, analogous to a
confirmation habeas corpus and the First Amendment,
safeguards personal equalities and propertyrights. The
first 29 articles of the constitution relate to pro-
tecting the right of amparo.

Voting is compulsory for all citizens (universal suf-
frage) over 18 years of age. This law is seldom enforced.

Supreme Court Members are appointed for life by the
President with the approval of the Senate. There are
21 members. The Supreme Court has four divisions: admi-
nistrative, civil, labor, and penal.

The parliament, National Congress, is a bicamaral
legislative body. The senate (Camara de Senadores) has
64 member, 2 from each state and 2 from the Federal
District. Each member serves a 6-year term. On the
Chamber of Deputies (Camara de Diputados) the membership

is considerably more complicated:

> The Chamber of Deputies consists of 230 members elected for three-year terms on the basis of one representative for each 200,000 people or fractions above 100,000, with minimum of two deputies from each state. There are also 37 at-large seats. Minority parties receiving a minimum of 1.5% of the national vote in a federal election are entitled, in addition to seats won outright, to five at-large seats in the Chamber plus one seat for each additional 0.5% of the votes polled up to a maximum of 25 seats for each party. Members of Congress are barred from reelection.[3]

The powers of Congress are abridged by the Executive Branch. The Congress enjoys no provision that would empower it to override a presidential veto. The powers tend to be relegated to a rubber stamping of presidential actions:

> The powers of Congress include ratification of treaties and conventions made with foreign powers, approval of judicial appointments of members to the Supreme Court and the superior courts, approval of the National Budget declarations of war and the establishment of schools.[4]

The state governments are unicameral. Muncipalities are the prevailing system of government at the local level. Members to the city government are elected by direct vote. Muncipalities are not allowed to pass tax legistlation. There are approximately 2300 muncipalities in Mexico.

The social system is generally stable with no racial problems. Mestizos are the ethnic majority with over 60 percent of the total population. The largest minority are Indians, comprising 30 percent of the population. The Mexican government provides certain incentives for the Indians to integrate into the Mexican culture.

Ninety percent of the Mexican population is Roman Catholic. This is a large proportion despite historical attempts to discourage strong Roman Catholic ties. Two era's stand out as antichurch (1867-72), (1910). The constitution reflects this influence.

---

[3] Arthur S. Banks, ed. Political Handbook of the World, 1979. (N.Y. McGraw-Hill Book Company, 1979) p. 300.

[4] Ibid.

6

ORGANIZATION OF THE MEXICAN GOVERNMENT

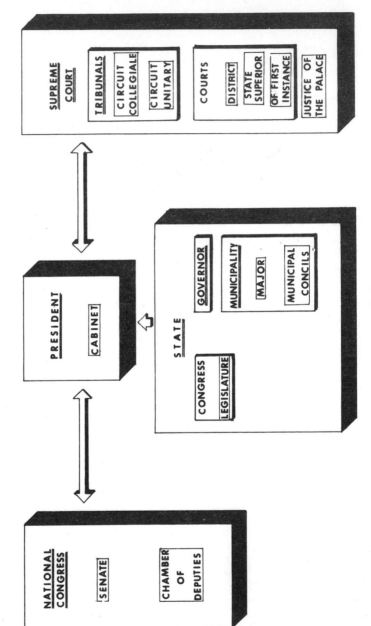

FIGURE 1.1

Ecclesiastical corporations have no legal rights
and theoretically cannot acquire property. reli
gious ceremonies cannot be held in public, and
all church buildings are considered national
property. The establishment of monastic orders
is prohibited. Ministries of religion must have
Mexican nationality; they have no political
rights and may not criticize the fundamental
laws of the country in either public or private
meetings.[5]

Many of these prohibitions have not been enforced as
many clergy have, in the mid 70's, allied themselves
with social concerns of the underprivileged.
The legal system derives from Spanish Civil Law,
which is very much a derivative of Roman Law that
places greater authority in the hands of magistrates.
The law is more from the top down and puts great power
in the hands of the prosecution, or state, through its
juridical decisions.

Social and Welfare Problems

Two government agencies are responsible for social
welfare programs in Mexico. The Mexican Institute of
Social Security and the Institute of Social Security and
Services for Government Employees. The first is responsi
ble for the private sector of the economy where it covers about 19 million workers and their dependents and
directly insures 3.5 million workers. The Institute of
Social Security and Service for Government serves 2 million federal and state personnel.

The programs offer three types of benefits: medical, economic, and social. Medical benefits include illness and maternity allowances and work-
men's compensation for occupational illnesses.
Economic benefits include sick pay, marriage expenses, old-age and disability pensions, funeral
expenses and pensions for widows and orphans. Social benefits include housing loans, vacation
centers and training programs.[6]

---

[5]G. Kurian, "Mexico", Encyclopedia of the Third World, Vol. II,
New York, 1978, P. 998.
[6]Ibid, p. 1002.

THE POPULATION

If we undertake the description of the evolution
process of the Mexican Population, it is sensible to
make the analysis starting from the year 1910. Looking
over the most relevant data, it is possible to distin-
guish four stages within this period. The first stage
that is from 1910 to 1940. The second is from 1940 to
1960. The third is from 1960 to 1970 and the last
from 1970 to date.

The Reconstruction Period (1910-1940)

The first period, which I have labeled "The Reconstruction Period" was marked by the outbreak of the
Mexican Revolution, the net effect of which was the loss
of more than a million human lives. Just to mention a
few figures, in 1910 the total population amounted to
15.1 million and by 1921 it was 14.4 million.[7] It was
not until three years later that the population level
of 15 million was reached again. From then onto 1940
the natural rate of population increase was approximately 1.6 per cent yearly. The population increase was
the result of a very high rate of fertility[8] (4.4 per
1000) and a very high rate of moratility (26 per 1000).
What justifies the label of "Reconstruction Period",
is that when the bloddy quarrels came to an end, social
stability was restored, an agrarian reform was set in
motion, and both the Central Bank and the Bank for
Economic Development (Nacional Financiera, S.A.) were
created in 1925[9] and 1934[10] respectively. It is also

---

[7] Migration to the United States was not then an important factor,
thus historian seem to agree that the loss in population was
mostly due to war and the lethal diseases that spread througout
the country in its wake.

[8] "Cuestiones Sociales", Comercio Exterior, Vol. 31, No. 10, Mexico
October 1981, p. 1110.

[9] The Central Bank was created by President Plutarco Elias Calles,
who is considered to be the last of the "Caudillos" who emerged
out of the Mexican Revolution.

[10] The creation of the Bank for Economic Development, and the nation
alization of the oil industry were both achieved by President
Lazaro Cardenas.

worth mentioning the nationalization of the Oil Industry
in 1938, later consolidated in a government controlled
monopoly corporation.

The Growth Period (1940-1960)

The year 1940 marked the beginning of an era in
which Mexico turned from a country of predominantly rural
population to one of urban population. In 1940 the population was 19.5 million[11] of which 35.1 percent were
living in urban areas and 64.9 percent were located in
rural areas. By the end of 1960 total population had
grown to 35 million and 50.7 percent of these were
urban dwellers mainly clustered in the five largest
metropolitan areas of Mexico city, Guadalajara, Monterrey, Ciudad Juarez, and Leon.
    Within this period the growth of population rose
sharply. The rate of population increase was about
2.1 percent per annum by 1940 and by 1960 it was estimated at 3.31[12] percent. The phenomena of urbanization
and demographic explotion that were experienced by Mexico during this period are attributed to the migration
flows from rural to urban areas[13] and to the sharp decline in the rate of mortality, which fell within this
period from 2.6[14] percent per annum to 0.3 percent. The
rate of fertility of 4.4 percent per annum remained
unchanged.

The Critical Period (1960-1970)

    This is the period during which demographic explo-
tion and rural migration to the cities reached their

---

[11]Secretaria de Programacion y Presupuesto (S.P.P.) Plan Global de
Desarrollo 1980-82, Mexico 1980, p. 127.

[12]
S.P.P., p. 127.

[13]
Cuestiones Sociales, "Comercio Exterior", Ed. Banco Nacional de
Comercio Exterior, México, October 1981, P. 1110.

[14]
The decline in the rate of mortality for the period under consideration it is believed to be the result of increased government investment in Public Health. In 1942 President Manuel Avila
Camacho creates the Social Security Institute to provide free
medicare for industrial workers. Today it has extended its
services to provide medical services for rural workers also.

peak.[15] Urban development became polarized in the sense that 2,000 small communities[16] of less than 2,500 inhabitants coexisted with a reduced number of large cities which accounted for almost 20 percent of total population.

The population for the five largest cities is presented in table 1.1

Table 1.1
Population in the Largest Mexican Cities

Area	Population 1960 000	1970 000	Rate of Growth %
Nation	38,746	53,358	3.5
Mexico City	5,080	8,540	5.2[16]
Guadalajara	608	1,131	6.2[17]
Monterrey	467	786	5.2[18]
Juarez City	236	410	5.5
Leon	173	359	7.3

The numerical results of Table 1.1 show that in 1960 the population of the five largest cities in Mexico represented almost 17 percent of the total population and by 1970 it was slightly above 21 percent. This growth of the cities can be partially explained by their high natural rate of growth and by the rural

---

[15]"Cuestiones Sociales", Comercio Exterior, p. 1110.

[16] P. Ramirez Vazquez, Mexico Vision de los Ochenta, Nina Menocal Eds., (Diana, 1st. Ed.), Mexico, August 1981, p. 235.

[17]"Cuestiones Sociales", Comercio Exterior, p. 1110.
[18]Ibid.

migration from the states of Hidalgo,[19] Oaxaca, Tlaxcala, Zacatecas, and to lesser extent from Coahuila, Tamaulipas, Chiapas, Durango, Guanajuato, Michoacan, Puebla and San Luis Potosi to the metropolitan areas of Table 1.1.

Newcomers, and old residents of the cities overtaxed available mass transportation systems, housing, hospitals, schools, univeristies and outgrew water and food supplies and the job creating capability of the largest urban centers.

The Recent Experience (1970-1981)

In the short-run the gloomy predictions of the seventies on population matter for Mexico, became a reality. By 1980 Greater Mexico City located 2400 meters (7200 feet) above the sea level had reached almost 14.5 million people[20] packed into an area of about half the size of New York City,[21] with a need of 50 cubic meters (150 cubic feet) of potable water per second. The water to be pumped from its source into Mexico City required one third of the electricity produced by "El Infiernillo" which is one of the most important hidroelectric system in the country.[22] Also the population distribution shown in diagram 2 portrays an expected large number of people in younger age groups.

In the long-run the Mexican population tends to stabilize slowly and to settle in a more even fashion all in different regions of the country. Cities linked to the oil industry such as Coatzacoalcos,[23] Minatitlan, Altamira and Villahermosa[24] are now powerful attraction

---

[19]"Cuestiones Sociales", Comercio Exterior, p. 1110.

[20]"Cuestiones Sociales", Comercio Exterior, p. 1113.

[21]Marline Simon, "The People Next Door", The Wilson Quarterly. Summer 1979, Vol. 3, No. 4, p. 123.

[22]P. Ramirez Vazquez, Mexico Vision de los Ochenta, p. 124.

[23]Carrada, F., El Mercado de Bienes Raices en Coatzacoalcos, ITESM, Mexico, June 1979, p. 73.

[24]Wade-Rovirosa L., "La Politica Demografica del Estado de Tabasco y su integración a la de Desarrollo", Boletin Informativo No. 5, National Council of Population, (CONAPO), Mexico, March 1981 P. 22-25.

12

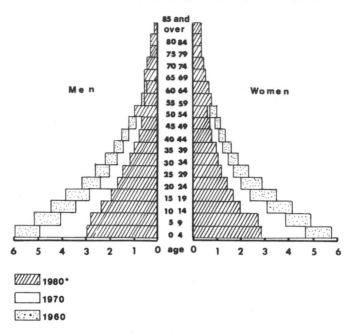

POPULATION PER QUINQUENNIAL AGE AND SEX GROUPS

*Estimate of the Consejo Nacional de Población (National Population Council)
SOURCE: Ninth General Population Census, D.S.P.P.

FIGURE 1.2

centers. Their natural rate of population increase was
6 percent per annum for the last decade, which was well
above the natural rate of growth of population of the
five largest cities for the same period. The metropoli
tan areas averaged a rate of growth of 4 percent per
annum, from 1970 to 1980 which is inferior to that shown
in the previous decade by the same cities.[25] Greater

---
[25]The rate of population increase for the five largest cities
during the period 1960-1970 was 4.5 percent per annum.

Mexico City for instance, showed a decline in the natural rate growth of population[26] from 5.2 percent in
1972 to 4.3 percent in 1980. Greater Monterrey declined
from 5.2 percent in 1970 to 3.5 percent in 1980; the
Metropolitan area of Guadalajara and the border towns
decreased from 3.2 percent to only 2.6 percent. At the
national level the natural rate of population increase
was 3.2 percent per annum in 1970, whereas in 1978 and
1979 it was 3.0 and 2.9 respectively and it is expected
to reach 2.5 percent for 1982.

The new information about the trend in the mexican
population prompted statisticians to change their fore-
casting about the future population outcome for the
nation and for the cities. The mexican population which
was 73 million in 1980 is expected to reach 100 million
by the year 2000. This forecast is lower than the previous one based on the population trend of the seventies.
By the end of the century Greater Mexico City is expected
to have 23 million people rather than 31 millions, which
would have been the expected number, had the fertility
rate and migrations flows remain unchanged.

An additional indication in the decline of natality
is the fact that the proportion of the age structure
between 0 and 4 years shrank from 16.9 percent of the
total population in 1970 to 14.2 percent in 1980.

Economically Active Population

From 1960 to 1980 significant shifts in labor force
distribution have taken place between sectors. Employment in the Agricultural sector dropped from 54.2 percent in 1960 to 32.2 percent in 1980. Services and
Construction showed an impressive gain from 13.5 to 30
and from 3.6 to 5 percent respectively for the same
period. A modest gain was made in manufacturing which
went from 15 to 18.6 percent, these shifts in labor
force distribution reflect both, the large migration
from rural to urban areas and the efforts undertaken by
the government to create new jobs. The outcome of the
effort was the creation of 3.25 million new jobs from
1978 to 1980.[27] The employment level reached 23 million

---

[26]G. Cabrera Acevedo, "Avances en el Cumplimiento de Objetivos
y Metas Demograficas y Desarrollo de Programas", Boletin Informativo No. 5, Conapo, Mexico, March 1981, p. 5-13.

[27]J. López Portillo, "Quinto Informe de Gobierno", Comercio
Exterior, Vol. 31, No. 9, Mexico, September 1981, P. 1047

14

in 1980.[28]

The impressive capability of the mexicans economy to create almost 700,000 new jobs year from 1978 to 1980 years has not been enough to overcome all the maladies associated with[29] underemployment and unemployment. Underemployment[30] is estimated to be 32 percent of the total employed labor force by 1980, and unemployment 5 percent for the same year. Structural underemployment of women is another problem. Women match men in the share of total population, but women are only 19 percent of the estimated 23 million labor force of 1980. Women are usually regarded as a reserve labor supply mainly as a result of the traditional attitude in the country toward women's role in society and to the reluctancy of employers to hire them.

7 of the[31] 23 million workers engaged in the labor force are members of some labor union and the rest remain unorganized, acting as free agents. The most important labor union in the country is the Confederation of Mexican Workers (CTM) which groups 3[32] million workers from which more than 5 percent[33] are agricultural workers and the rest industrial workers.

This important labor union with a membership of 600,000 workers in 1937 was founded by the leftist leader Vicente Lombardo Toledano who was succeded by Fidel Velazquez who has remained in power for more than 30 years. This influential leader has played a key role in Mexican politics since his arrival to the leadership of the CTM.

In Table 1.2 below is shown the behavior of economically active population from 1960 to 1980.

---

[28] J. López Portillo, "Quinto Informe de Gobierno", Comercio Exterior, Vol. 31, No. 9, Mexico, September 1981, P. 1047.

[29] A worker is classified as underemployed when he does not get all year round the minimum wage of the area where he lives. A typical example is the agricultural worker who receives the minimum wage only during the agricultural cycle, and receives nothing in the interim.

[30] P. Ojeda Paullada, Mexico Vision de los Ochenta, P. 169.

[31] F. Velázquez, Mexico Vision de los Ochenta, P. 142.

[32] Ibid.

[33] Ibid.

Table 1.2
Economically Active Population, 1960-1980

	1960		1975		1980	
	000	%	000	%	000	%
Labor Force	11,332	100	16,597	100	23,000	100
Of which:						
Agriculture, Livestock Forestry, Hunting & Fishing	6,144	54.2	6,778	40.9	7,306	32.2
Mining & Extractive Industries	142	1.3				
Manufacturing	1,556	13.7			4,278	18.6
Construction	408	3.6	763	4.6	1,150	5.0
Electricity, Gas	41	0.4	66	0.4	100	0.5
Commerce	1,075	9.5	1,660	10.0	2,530	11.0
Transport	375	3.1	498	3.0	600	3.0
Services	1,527	13.5	3,668	22.1	6,900	29.5
Raw Classified	82	0.7	763	0.4	400	0.2

Sources: Statistics on the Mexican Economy. 1964, Banco de Comercio 1975,
5° Informe de Gobierno 1980.

RECENT ECONOMIC PERFORMANCE

Mexico's GDP has been growing at relative large rates when compared to many other LDCs. Between 1940 and 1960 Mexico was very much in the limelight of international attention for its rapid growth rates. During that time the Mexican GDP had increased from 21.7 billion pesos to 74.3 billion pesos. This was an annual increase of 6.4 percent.[34] during the 1960s the momentum continued at a slower rate, averaging 4.6 percent per annum.[35] Table 1.3 below gives recent trends in the GDP.

Table 1.3
Trends in the Gross Domestic Product

Total (Pesos)	1975	1976	1977	1978	1979
Current Prices	1,000.9	1,220.8	1,640.0	2,104.6	2,733.8
Constant (1975)					
prices	1,000.9	1,022.2	1,053.0	1,122.5	1,225.8
Real Increase (%)	4.1	2.1	3.0	6.6	7.2
Per Capita (Pesos)					
Current prices	16,640	19,586	25,390	31,440	39,403
Constant (1975)					
prices	16,640	16,400	16,269	16,769	17,336
Real Increase (%)	0.7	-1.4	-0.8	3.1	3.4

Source: IMF International Financial Statistics

---

[34] Peter H. Smith, "The Wounds of History, "The Wilson Quarterly, summer 1979, (Vol. 3, No. 4, P. 136.

[35] The Economist Intelligence Unit Ltd., Quarterly Economic Review of Mexico, Annual Supplement 1979.

By the governments own estimate Gross Domestic Product increased during 1980 by 8.3 percent due to a surge in export earnings from oil and gas. The further development of oil and gas promises to allow Mexico to move its economic development pace at considerably more rapid rates than even in the past.

More recent data shows the relative decline of agriculture, forestry, hunting and fishing as a percentage of GDP over a five year period.

Expenditures patttern in Table 1.4 display an enlargement of government expenditure relative to private expenditure.

Table 1.4
Expenditure Generating Gross Domestic Product
(At current prices)

	1972		1977		1979	
	bn pesos	%	bn pesos	%	bn pesos	%
Government Consumption	43.7	8.5	216.9	13.2	317.0	11.5
Private consumption	375.0	73.2	1,090.0	66.6	1,724.8	62.5
Fixed capital formation	98.0	19.1	328.6	20.0	698.1	25.2
Increase in stocks	0.2	-	5.0	0.3	75.5	2.7
Exports of goods & services	45.5	8.9	167.5	10.2	342.0	12.3
Less imports of goods $ services	50.2	-9.7	-168.5	-10.3	-390.4	-14.2
Gross domestic product	512.3	100.0	1,659.5	100.0	2,767.0	100.0

Source: IMF International Financial Statistics.

The proportion of Gross Domestic Product consumed by government increased 35 percent from 1972 to 1979, while the proportion of the pie that went to private consumption fell by 10.7 percent. The proportion of exports increased 38 percent, mainly as a result of the growth of crude oil exports. In 1976 exports earnings on petroleum reached 1.7[36] billion. In 1981 they are expected to reach $19 billion[37]. This is more than total exports of $5.1 billion in 1978 and of $7.7 billion in 1979.[38]

---

[36] Economist's Intelligence Unit, Annual Supplement 1979, P. 12.

[37] M. de la Madrid, Mexico Vision de los Ochenta, 1981, P. 34

[38] Economist's Intelligence Unit, First Quarter, 1980, P. 11.

Fueled by increased revenues from the oil sector, the growth of Gross National Product was in real terms 9.2 and 8.3 percent in 1979 and 1980[39] respectively.

Composition of Gross Domestic Product (GDP)

Manufacturing and trade are the largest segments of GDP. However, during the period 1970 to 1975 the greatest growth rates were in transportation and construction. Table 1.5 shows the proportion of GDP in certain areas.

Table 1.5
Origin of Gross Domestic Product

| Activity | YEAR | | | |
| | 1972 | | 1979 | |
	bn pesos	%	bn pesos	%
Agriculture, Forestry, Hunting,	52.9	10.3	164.5	9.8
fishing	52.9	10.3	164.5	9.8
Mining & quarrying	18.9	3.7	86.0	5.1
Manufacturing	120.2	23.6	399.9	23.9
Construction	27.3	5.3	99.1	5.9
Electricity, gas & water	7.3	1.4	24.2	1.4
Transport, storage & communications	14.6	2.8	53.1	3.2
Wholesale & retail trade	162.4	31.7	446.5	27.8
Other services	108.7	21.2	382.8	22.9
Gross Domestic Product	512.3	100.0	1,679.0	100.0

Agriculture. In most recent years, the rate of growth of the Mexican agriculture output has been of great concern. Mexico has experienced a decrease in self-sufficiency on increase in imports of agricultural products. At least in 1979 part of this increase in agricultural imports can be explained by poor weather.

One major problem regarding agricultural self-sufficiency is the transportation problem within Mexico. Infrastructure is lacking to enable quick and cheap transportation of agricultural commodities to the urban

---

[39]"Recuento Nacional", Comercio Exterior, Vol. 31, No. 10, Mexico Oct. 1981, P. 1113.

areas. This inadequacy of transportation has played
havoc with the Mexican government's efforts to restrain
the rise in price of food products.

The transportation problem is not just an internal
problem. Mexico has considerable problems in main-
taining adequate distribution channels for imported food
stuffs as well. Inadequate port facilities, poor quality roads and inadequate storage facilities compound
the problems.[40]

Another of the more distressing aspects of Mexico's
agriculture production is that it is failing to increase
in proportion to the increase in population. Between
1970 and 1974 agricultural production[41] increased by
less than one percent per annum, compared with population growth of 3.5 percent per annum. In 1976 the
volume of output fell and rose slightly in 1977 and 1978
just to fell badly again in 1979 and rise again in 1980.

Some have argued among others the Mexican President
Jose Lopez Portillo,[42] that a large part of this unsatis-
factory performance of the agricultural sector can be
attributed to an overemphasis upon industrial growth and
a general feeling among government planners that expenditure for infrastructure in rural areas was simply of
low priority.[43] Regardless of this possible neglect of
the rural communities, the drift of population from
rural areas to urban areas poses considerable challenge
to planners to accomodate the increasing urban popu-
lations. As mentioned earlier, and also to deal with
the politics of food imports in a country plenty of
natural resources.

---

[40] U.S. Foreign Service in Mexico, Foreign Economic Trends and Their
Implications for the U.S. (Washington, D.C.).

[41] E.I.U., Annual Supplement, P. 7.

[42] J. López Portillo, "9° Informe de Gobierno," Comercio Exterior,
Vol. 31, No. 9, Mexico, September 1981, P. 1050.

[43] "Mexico has about 82,000 rural communities with fewer than 2,500
inhabitants, and they seem to rank low on the government's list of
priorities. Planners argues that it takes too much money to bring
water, electricity, and roads to such small communities." For
further comments see Ramirez Vazquez P., Mexico Vision de los
Ochenta, Nina Menocal Ed., Diana Ediciones, Mexico, August 1981,
P. 235.

Supposedly 48 percent of Mexico's land area is considered agricultural, but only 12 percent of the land
area is under cultivation,[44] and agriculture employed
32.2 percent of the labor contributing a mere 10 percent
to total GDP and 9 percent of export earnings in 1981.[45]
The government has taken remedial steps recently to
encourage agricultural development. In 1979, and into
1980, the Mexican government imposed an export limitation on beef to lower the price of beef to the domestic population. On the surface this may seem contrary
to development of the agricultural sector, and it may
well be. But one can trace ways that this might help
the agriculture sector. First, it is very likely that
export restrictions would tend to lower the price that
beef growers would receive and discourage them from
growing cattle. Depending on whether beef cattle are
raised on mainly cultivatable land, this would be a plus
for increased supplies of other farm products. Cattle
growers would convert their land holdings to the production of food stuffs, and therefore increase the
availability of agriculture products and lower the
price through increased supply. But if the land is
suitable for only grazing, then this policy would very
well be counter productive, driving even more people to
the urban areas.
Some price supports have been initiated to increase
farm incomes and to stem the tide of rural-to-urban
migration.[46] The specifics of the proposed price supports have been formulated within the context of the
plan known as the Alimentary Mexican System (SAM).
Mexican agriculture is typified by three different
types of land holding: private communal and public.
Particularly unique to Mexico is its ejidos, or system
of communal land holdings that dates back to pre-con-
quest times. There are at least 14,000 ejidos comprising 40 percent of the cultivated land. Management
of the ejidos is by election and they are recognized
as corporations. The ejidatario, or farm laborer on the
ejidos has the right to farm a maximum of 10 hectars of

[44]George Kurian, ed., Encyclopedia of the Third World (New York:
Facts on File, 1978) P. 994.

[45]J. Velázquez Toledo, "Sumario Estadístico", Comercio Exterior,
Vol. 35, No. 9 Mexico, September 1981, P. 1091.

[46]"Mexico Tries To Slice Its Cake So That Everygone Gets A Share"
World Business Weekly, (June 2, 1980) P. 22.

irrigated land and 20 hectores of dry land. An ejido
must be worked within at least 2 consecutive years or
the ejidataro's assigned land is taken back by the ejidos administration and assigned to another. This communal system of land holding is subject to much contro-
versy as to its economic efficiency. Arguments against
the system are based largely upon the tendency for there
to be considerable seperation between ones efforts and
the rewards he receives. Also, some argue that not
allowing private ownership tends to weaken ones at-
tachment to the soil and therefore his lack of regard
for careful husbandry. Proponents usually argue that
the system is more egalitarian.

Private ownership of land is limited to a maximum of
100 hectars. However, a sizeable number have managed
to circumvent this limitation since there are about 500
private farms with over 50,000, and more than 40,000
farms over 101 hectars.

Efforts at land reform have been met with rather
poor results. Distribution of production is still very
unequal. Of more than 2.8 million farms, 4 percent account for 50 percent of agricultural production; about
1 percent produce all of the agricultural exports, and
about 15 percent produces most of the food for urban
areas.

Between 1976 and 1981, 14.13 million hectars
(34.9 million acres) were distributed to 224,000
farmers.[49]

A major agriculture support industry just recently
providing tangible results is the fertilizer industry.
Mexico's Guanos y Fertilizantes Mexicanos built two
area plants having a combined capacity of 825,000 tons
annually.[50] A new plant at Pajaritos will have a capacity of 495,000 tons annually.[51] Several other
fertilizer plants stand in line for construction, two
ammonium sulphate plants at Queretaro with a capacity
for each of 200,000 tons per year.

[47] George Kurian Ed., Encyclopedia of the Third World (New York:
Facts on File, 1978) P. 995.

[48] Ibid

[49] J. López Portillo, 5° Informe de Gobierno" Comercio Exterior,
Vol. 31, No. 9, Mexico, September 1981, P. 1050.

[50] E.I.U., Annual Supplement, 1979, P. 15.

[51] E.I.U., Annual Supplement, 1979, P. 15.

Corn is Mexico's biggest food crop. Nearly one half
of all crop land is given to the production of maize for[52]
which Mexico is the 15th largest producer in the world.
One third of the land is pasture. Due to the vast pasture land, Mexico is one of the world's largest beef
producers and beef exporters. Table 1.6 below gives
the total quantities of crops produced in Mexico from
1973/74 to 1979/1980.

Table 1.6
Production of Principal Agricultural Products

	1974/75	1975/76	1976/77	1977/78	1978/79
Maize	8,459	8,945	10,714	10,909	8,752
Wheat	2,798	3,354	2,456	2,643	2,272
Cotton	215	213	416	340	337
Coffee	230	212	182	270	228
Sugar Cane	35,841	31,387	30,390	30,000	35,415
Rice	717	463	567	397	487
Beans	1,027	740	762	940	552

an estimate
Sources: Secretaria de Agricultura y Ganaderia,
Ministry of Planning and the Budget, cited in
E.I.U., Annual Supplement, 1979, P. 10
Also, Banco de Mexico, Informe Anual, 1980 P 73,
5° Informe de Gobierno, September, 1981.

The only clear trend which emerges from the information of Table 1.6 is the declining output of sugar.
This might be due to the softening of the world market
for sugar.
Mexico's coastal exposure is large and fishing output is therefore considerable. From the Table 1.7 one

[52] J. López Portillo, "5° Informe de Gobierno", Comercio
Exterior, P. 1051.

is struck by the large decline in fish catch from 1977
to 1980 when shrimp catch declined by 95.1 percent,
oyster by 25.9 percent and tuna by 15.8 percent.
Hopefully this is merely a short run aberration since
a young growing population requires a rich protein
source, and already many are malnourished. Only one
third of Mexico's[53] million people can afford adequate
diets and some 40 percent suffer from outright malnutri-
tion.

Mexico has a large potential in forestry. An estimated 20 percent of Mexico's land is forested, mostly
in Chihuahua, Durango and Michoacan. Only 25 percent
of Mexico's potential 385 million cubic meters of timber
is now exploited.[54]

In terms of foreign trade, agriculture contributed
less than 10 percent of total export value by 1981.
Table 1.7 displays the comparison of main products exported from 1977 to 1980 in U.S. dollars.

Table 1.7
Main Products Exported by Mexico
($000,000)

	1977	1978	1979	1980
Crude Petroleum	890.9	1,663.3	3,764.6	9,429.6
Coffee	454.3	329.4	531.5	415.2
Cotton	77.8	114.1	309.3	320.9
Shrimps	162.0	78.2[a]	23.1	7.8
Cattle	23.6	81.8	104.5	76.7
Fresh or Frozen Meat	45.4	71.9		
Flourspar	39.7	53.3		

Source: Banco de Mexico, Informe Anual 1980, P. 177

Agriculture products have become a smaller proportion
of total export value due to the burgeoning petroleum
sector. The cattle exports increase is most striking
and might be considered one of the factors which precip-
itated export limitations on beef during 1979 and 1980.

1979 was a very poor year for the agriculture sector.
Drought hit areas not irrigated, delivering less than
18 percent the average rainfall. Basic foods were struck
severely despite efforts to increase output.

---

[53] Marlise Simons, "The People Next Door," The Wilson Quarterly (summer 1979), Vol. 3, No. 4, P. 129.
[54] E.I.U., Annual Supplement, 1979, P. 11.

Even though 940,000 extra hectores were planted
last year, fertilizer usage increased by 12 percent and there was wide introduction of improved
seeds, the harvests of basic food crops fell
sharply. The maize crop,at 8.9 mn tons, was 2
mn tons down on the previous year, creating the
need for substantial imports (2.7 mn tons) in
1980). The bean harvest was 32 percent lower
than in 1978, yielding only 638,000   tons and
implying a need for 250,000 tons of imports this
year.[55]

By 1980, when rainfall was on time and the government support program to the agricultural sector was
abundant, a record crop of 24,000,000[56] tons of basic
grains were gathered.[57] This crop was superior 11 percent to that of 1978[58] which reached the level of
21,178,000 tons. It was also almost 30 percent above
the crop of 1970.

The government support program was a package which
included as economic measures, a sharp increase in the
price of guarantee of the basic grains, an abundant
government supplied improved seed and fertilizers

In spite of all this effort, Mexico's agriculture
sector which stands as one of its most important sector
is in a more serious condition. Population growth has
more than outstepped gains made in agriculture production in the last decade due to the poor marketing
transportation system and the neglect shown by planners
in the past regarding agriculture infrastructure develop
ment.

Industry.   One can gain some idea about the
structure of the Mexican industry by the proportion of
GDP that each sector contributes and by the proportions
of the working population employed in each. Table 1.8
shows the proportions contributed by each sector to the
GDP for 1972 and 1977 and the changes in this proportion.
Significant increased occurred in mining, quarrying,
transportation, storage and communications. The largest

---

[55] E.I.U., 1st Quarter 1980, P. 16.

[56] J. López Portillo, "5° Informe de Gobierno", Comercio Exterior,
Vol. 9, P. 1051.

[57] Ibid.

[58] Ibid.

drop occurred in wholesale and retail trade. The rural
to urban migration might partially be accountable for
the decrease in proportion contributed by the sector,
agriculture, forestry, hunting and fishing.

Table 1.8
Industrial Origin of Gross Domestic Product[a]
(at current prices)

	1972		1977	
	bn pesos	%	bn pesos	%
Agriculture, forestry, hunting & fishing	52.9	10.3	164.5	9.0
Mining & quarrying	18.9	3.7	86.0	5.1
Manufacturing	120.2	23.6	399.9	23.9
Construction	27.3	5.3	99.1	5.9
Electricity, gas & water	7.3	1.4	24.2	1.4
Transport, storage & communications	14.6	2.8	53.1	3.2
Wholesale & retail trade	162.4	31.7	466.5	27.8
Other services	108.7	21.2	382.8	22.9
Gross domestic product	512.3	100.0	1,676.0	100.0

a There is a slight discrepancy betwen IMF and UN figures
  for GDP in 1977.

Source: UN Monthly Bulletin of Statistics.

Table 1.2 sheds light upon the relative sector
employment responsible for the above mentioned GDP con-
tributions. Unfortunately Table 1.2 and 1.8 do not coin-
cide chronologically. But taken together, and assuming
that changes are not too significant in the 1975-77
labor proportions they do suggest the relative productivity of each sector. Labor employed in agriculture,
livestock, forestry, hunting and fishing would appear to
be very low in over all productivity. Here approximately 40 percent of the economically active population was
contributing approximately a mere 10 percent of the GDP,
an output to labor ratio of only .24. By comparison the
ratios of manufacturing and mining, construction, and
electricity, gas and water are respectively 1.6, 1.28,
and 3.5.[59]

_____
[59]D. Miller, Mexico: Country Report, Working Paper, University of
  Colorado, Boulder, 1978, P. 28.

The rates of change of main sectors of industry from year-to-year in the recent years developed a great robust quality (Table 1.9). From the years 1976 to 1980 only two changes in the indexes for the various industrial sectors were negative

Table 1.9
Industrial Production (1976-1980)

	1976	1977	1978	1979	1980
Manufactures	142.9	147.8	162.5	174.3	184.06
(% of change)		3.6	10.0	9.8	5.6
Petroleum	153.6	178.8	200.3	222.7	261.6
(% of change)		16.4	15.1	15.9	17.5
Petrochemicals	192.9	185.1	218.5	223.2	249.9
(% of change)		-4.0	18.0	10.0	12.0
Mining	119.4	120.3	122.9	125.9	134.08
(% of change)		.8	2.1	1.5	6.5
Electricity	169.2	184.9	200.1	210.7	224.4
(% of change)		9.3	9.0	8.6	6.5
Construction	147.5	144.5	163.7	176.6	199.2
(% of change		-2.4	13.3	14.3	12.8

Source: U.S. State Department, Foreign Economic Trends and Their Implications for the U.S. 1979 May, 1980 Jan.
Banco de Mexico, Informe Anual, 1980, P. 60.

The two down turns recorded could have been, in part, due to the jarring of the money devaluation of 1976. The largest single year-to-year change was recorded between 1977 and 1978 in the petrochemical sector at 18 percent. Growth in petrochemicals is targeted to allow greater increase of output in the agriculture sector.
Electricity production was expected to continue its high rate of growth since the Federal Electricity Commission (CFE) announced plans to accelerate the plant construction program in order to meet an anticipated growth in demand for electrical energy of 13 percent a year from 1979 to 1982. [60] The results however have been a steady decline in the rate of growth after 1977.

---

[60] U.S. Foreign Service, "Mexico" Foreign Economic Trends and Their Implications for the United States, January 1980, P. 5.

Mexico's auto industry has been booming. Production rose 33% during 1978 and had increased during the first six months of 1979 by 19 percent.[61] Expected production rate for 1979 will exceed 400 thousand units. Production levels of tractor trailers actually doubled in the first six months of 1979. This output is the product of seven auto companies, with Volkswagen leading the production level in 1979.[62]

Mexico has one of the oldest iron and steel industries of Latin America. Output increase were impressive in the first six months of 1979, growing by 9 percent.[63] In 1978 the growth in production reached 20 percent.[64] These large increases in production were in part fueled by significant demands made upon the sector by petrochemical, petroleum and manufacturing sectors. Even so the steel industry was not producing at full capacity due to labor problems at some locations and bottlenecks in receiving raw materials.[65]

Construction activity increased from 1976 to 1980 9.5 percent driven by government contracts which frequently accounts for more than half of construction projects undertaken in Mexico.[66] A storage of cement resulted in action by the government to authorize imports and to restrict exports of cement and to encourage public and private investment in this area.

Mexico is somewhat protectionist. This is one of the main reasons it has not signed the General Agreement on Tariffs and Trade (GATT) in early 1980.[67] Some cabinet members of the Mexican government favored membership in GATT but strong anti-GATT lobbyists exerted influence in dissuading[68] President Lopez Portillo from joining

---

[61]D. Miller, Mexico: Country Report, P. 31.

[62]Ibid

[63]Kurian, p. 996.

[64]Foreign Service, January 1980, P. 5.

[65]Ibid.

[66]Ibid, P. 6.

[67]"Economic Digest: Mexico" World Business Weekly (April 7, 1980), P. 27.

[68]"In March of 1980 Mexican President Jose Lopez Portillo announced two key factors of his new economic policy: first that Mexico would not join the GATT, and secondly, that the growth of crude oil production would be limited a 10 percent increase per year. This decision was interpreted in Mexico as a personal achievement of Jose Andres de Oteyza, Secretary of Government properties and Industrial Development", wrote Menocal Nina, Mexico Vision de los Ochenta, Ed. Diana, Mexico, August 1980, P. 138.

since they argued that liberalization of trade policies
would result in more harm than good. However, Mexico
has participated in the Tokyo Round negotiations and are
set upon abiding by GATT though not exceeding the status
of a signatory.

Mexico has an insignifcant quantity of imported
labor and welcomes new technology. Imported technology
is permitted under the "Law to Promote Mexican Investment and to Regulate Foreing Investment" of 1973. Es-
sentially this law provides that:

> Foreign investments are welcomed under certain
> conditions, such as when the compliment domes-
> tic investment, introduce new technology, help
> to increase exports and import substitution,
> use a high percentage of local components, are
> labor intensive and are located in a depressed
> area of the country.[69]

Transportation and Communication Infrastructures.

One of Mexico's major stumbling blocks to smooth
continuous economic growth is its insufficient internal
transportation system. Though extensive it remains
inadequate in view of present needs and anticipated future requirements. In 1975 the Mexican rail system
consisted of:

> An integrated network of six lines with a total
> length of 15,100 km (9,378 mi). Five of the six
> lines are owned by the government. The largest,
> National Railways, operates about 70 percent of
> the total trackage and carries about 80 percent
> of the total traffic.[70] The second largest is
> the Pacific Railroad linking Nogales with Guada
> lajara. Both these railways are autonomous
> government agencies. The three other government
> lines are Chihuahua to Pacific Railroad, the
> Sonora-Baja California Railroad and United Rail
> roads of the Southeast. The rail system links
> with the United States at several points, such
> as at Ciudad Juarez, Laredo, Piedras Negras,
> Reynosa, Matamoros, Nogales, Naco and Agua Prie

---

[69]Kurian, P. 996.

[70]Mexico City Chamber of Commerce, Mexico 1980, September 1980,
P. 72.

ta and with Central America through Guatemala.
A short stretch of 102 km (63 mi) is electri-
fied. An underground railway system was opened
in Mexico City in 1969. Rail traffic in 1975
consisted of 4,198 billion passenger-km and
32,542 billion net-tone-km."71

The problems with insufficient railroads was made
clear in 1979 at the Texas-Mexican border when railway
freight congestion became so bad that "every siding from
Laredo to the Oklahoma border - distance of some 500
miles - was backed up for a time with Mexican-bound
cargo."72

The railroad problems are numerous:

The 12,500 miles of track is old and not elec-
trified, gradients are generally steep, engines
are unrealiable, and because there is no com-
putarization, freight cars often cannot be
traced in the system. A quarter of the workers
are past the retirement age, but Ferrocarriles
Nacionales, the state railway company, is already paying pensions of more than $1 billion
and cannot pay any more. However, this year the
government is supposed to assume the railway's
pension73 obligations, thus enabling the company to retire74 its older employees.

So almost with saying, the Mexican government plans
to invest considerable money and effort into renovating
its railroad system:

It plans to electrify the track on the busiest
routes and lay 375 miles of new track before
the turn of the century. The state rail construction company recently signed a 10 year,
$480 million contract with GE of the U.S. to

71Kurian, P. 997.

72"Mexico: A Stumbling Transport System", World Business Weekly,
June 30, 1980, P. 22.

73President Lopez Portillo announced in his 5th delivery to the
nation that after 1981 pensions of retired workers in Mexico will
increase in the same proportion than do wages and salaries of
active workers.

74"Mexico: A Stumbling Transport System", World Business Weekly,
June 30, 1980, P. 22.

deliver up to 100 new locomotives per year,
the contract gives Mexico the option to as-
semble some of the components itself. There
are also plans to add 3,500 freight cars to
Mexico's rolling stock this year, compares
with 588 added[75] last year, 1979.

Mexico's internal transportation problems do not
stop with the railroads. Trucking inefficiency poses
another challenge. Since only one quarter of Mexico's
freight is moved by rail, and since no system of barge
lines exist, a sizeable part of the remainder must be
moved by truck. But the trucking industry is bound by
special interests. Many politicians derive great bene-
fit from the partial, or complete, ownership of government fixed routes. These routes are not easily changed
since changes may infringe upon another's monopolized
service area. As it is now, the truck transportation
is unsuited to accomodate Mexico's rapid rate of economic growth.[76]
"Mexican port facilities will have to be expanded
to handle the tremendous increase in its share of world
commerce brought about by its newly found petroleum
wealth. Ocean port activity is very concentrated: Five
of Mexico's 49 ocean ports - Tampico, Veracruz, Guaymas,
Mazatlan, and Manzanillo - handle 80% of the nation's
ocean freight. [77]
Though truck freight transportation is hamstrung by
certain privileges of an institutional nature, the road
system itself is one of the best in Latin America. Mexi[78-]
co has over 209,780 (130,487 mi) of all weather roads
(of which 68% are paved) Roads reach 40% of national
territory.[79]
Mexico has a large number of domestic airlines, 77
in all with only two being international: Aeromexico
and Mexicana. The government owns 100% of Aeromexico
and 10% of Mexicana. There are about 1,768 airfields
besides the the airport facilities of Mexico City

-----

[75]Ibid, P. 23.

[76]World Business Weekly, June 2, 1980, P. 23.

[77]Kurian, P. 998.

[78]Mexico City Chamber of Commerce, Mexico 1980, P. 29.

[79]Kurian, P. 998.

of which 717 are useable, 135 have permanent surface
runways, and 22 have runways over 2,500 meters (8,000
ft.).[80]

Petroleum. As pointed out earlier, oil discoveries
appeared to be the key to the economic upsurge of the
Mexican economy during the last three years, and have
brightened the economic capabilities of the country;
thus it seems convenient to examine the oil sector to
better understand today's economic conditions in Mexico.
The priest Dn. Manuel Gil y Saenz discovered in Te-
pepitlan, Tabasco, in 1863,[81] a natural oil well that
was later named "Mina de Petroleo de Sn. Fernando," from
which oil was extracted commercially for the first time
in Mexico. Mr. Gil exported ten barrels of oils to New
York, the quality of which was accepted. However, by
then oil prices had fallen from 20 dollars to 10 cents
in the United States,[82] and this made oil exports to the
United States unprofitable. The well was later under
the management of Mr. Simon Sarlat who tried to sell the
product on the national market. However, the lack of
adequate communications between Tepetitlan and the consumer center in Mexico City discouraged further exploration of the well, in spite of the acute shortage of
the product then, which was used to provide domestic il-
lumination.
Eighteen years later, in Papantla, Veracruz, Dr.
Adolph Autrey, who was Irish, announced another natural
oil well that was named "La Constancia" from which was
naturally extracted petroleum for purposes of illumina-
tion.
In 1901 "La Ley del Petroleo"[83] was issued which
granted powers to the federal government to authorize con
cessions to exploit privately oil resources within land
under the ownership of the federal government. This law
also granted rights to private citizens to exploit oil
resources on their properties according to their wishes.
Pearson, a former partner of Dr. Sarlat, taking
advantage of the possibilities opened by the new law,
founded the company "El Aguila" that first exploited the

---

[80]Kurian, P. 998

[81]J.D. Lanvin, Petroleo, Ed. Fondo de Cultura, Mexico, 1980, P. 12.

[82]The dramatic fall in oil price was the result of a new technique
of oil wells tried by Col. Drake in 1858 which greatly improved
the available oil supply in the United States.

[83]Lavin, P. 51.

oil resources in Mexico, opening the first drill well in
1960.[84] In 1931, the Royal Dutch bought stock in El
Aguila and gained control over it.

In the early twenties, Standard Oil gained control
over some of the "Mexican" companies already in operation on the "golden line."[85]

In 1935,[86] the first legally recognized oil labor
union was born. In 1937 a strike called by the oil
labor union was set in motion. To mend the rift between
the workers and the oil companies, the case was taken to
the Supreme Court which ruled in favor of the labor
union petitions. The oil companies openly refused to
accept this ruling and widened the battleground to the
international arena. The Mexican President, Gral. Lazaro Cardenas, attempting to temper this conflict, called
a meeting with the representatives of the oil companies.
In light of a new refusal on the part of the oil companies to accept the ruling of the Supreme Court, Presi-
dente Lazaro Cardenas abruptly expropriated the oil
companies to further consolidate them in a government-
owned industry called "Petroleos Mexicanos," on June
17th, 1938.[87] Its board of directors was integrated by
nine members.

When the oil industry was nationalized in 1938,
proven reserves were estimated at 821 million barrels.
The output of the oil industry then amounted to 105,389
barrels per day,[88] of which 9.16 million barrels (total
per year) were exported at an average price of 0.98
United States dollars per barrel. Total sales of Petroleos Mexicanos (PEMEX) amounted to 154.9 million pesos
for that year, of which 18.4 million[89] were paid as
taxes to the federal government. The upsurge of world
oil prices in 1973 encouraged geological research in
Mexico that very soon paid dividends in terms of probable and proven reserves. In 1981, according to PEMEX
officials, proven reserves have climbed to the astonish-
ing amount of 73 billion barrels, and probable reserves
are believed to be over 250 billion barrels.[90] At the

---

[84]Ibid, P. 57.

[85]An area that runs along the coast of the Gulf of Mexico, where
the first giant oil field in Mexico was discovered.

[86]P.F. Ortiz, Petroleo y Soberania, Ed. Posadas, S.A., Mexico 1979,
P. 394.

[87]In a decree issued on that date by the executive power and af-
firmed by the Mexican Congress.

[88]Lavin, P. 272.

[89]J. López Portillo, "5° Informe de Gobierno", Comercio Exterior.
P. 1056
[90]E.I.U, 1980, First Quarter.

same time that the world oil price was growing, the Mexican oil reserves did so too. Mexico in 1981 was pricing
its crude oil exports at an average of 31.25 Unites
States dollars per barrel.[91] Mexico exported 1,100,000
barrels per day in 1981 mainly to the United States,[92]
Israel and Spain. Oil exports to these countries altogether amounted to more than 90 percent of total Mexican exports.

In spite of all these bright expectations and the
international pressure -through diplomatic channels- to
increase the rate of production more rapidly, the govern
ment seems to have adopted a cautious attitude of "go
slowly and plan". This attitude is reflected in the set-
ting up of a desired target of a 2.25 million barrel per
day rate,[93] and a future rate of growth of 10 percent
necessary to cover the domestic demand for energy that
has been increasing at a rate of 7.1 percent[94] per annum. Energy in Mexico is basically provided by petroleum consumption. However, conservative the attitude
of the Mexican government may be so far, the tremendous
rate of growth of oil production during the last five
years has required both a rise in imports to provide the
required capital goods for extraction purposes, and an
increase in export revenues for PEMEX that for 1981
is expected to reach 15 billion U.S. dollars, which is
superior in 50 percent to the amount exported in 1980
which amounted to 10 billion U.S. dollars.[95] Taxes paid
by PEMEX to the federal government have risen tremendously to the amount of 319.2 billion pesos for 1981.
All this implies that the development of PEMEX, has
given it current economic importance in the economy as
a whole and on the overall balance of payments, not only
because of all the physical imports and exports of this
industry, but also because of all the positive expectations that it creates. It also has an important
impact in overall government revenues. Taxes paid by
PEMEX provides in 1981 28 percent of total government
revenues.

Petroleum production in Mexico can be seen from the
Table 1.10 below.

[91] J. López Portillo, P. 1054.
[92] Ibid.
[93] J. Diaz, Informe Anual de PEMEX, Mexico 1979.
[94] H. Castillo, Petroleo y Soberania, Editorial Posada, P. 205.
[95] J. López Portillo, P. 1054

Table 1.10
Petroleum Production Rates in Mexico, 1968-1980
(Millions of barrels per day)

YEAR	EXTRACTION	YEAR	EXTRACTION
1968	440.0	1975	806.0
1969	461.0	1976	897.0
1970	487.0	1977	1,086.0
1971	486.0	1978	1,330.0
1972	507.0	1979	1,440.0
1973	525.0	1980	2,350.0

Source: PEMEX 1981, figure Hammond Almanac, 1980;
1980 figure World Business Weekly, April 7, 1980,
P. 17.

Uranium. Surprising to many, Mexico, a country ex-
traordinarily well endowed with natural energy deposits
plans to develop a nuclear alternative. The prospects
of Mexico going nuclear are bolstered by Mexico's large
quantities of proven uranium resources, 10,000 metric
tons and as much as 250,000 tons of potential reserves[96]
Uramex, the Mexican uranium[97] company is planning to
build its first processing plant at Perra Blanca, Chihua
hua, with an annual production capacity of 400 metric
tons of enriched uranium. The first of two light water
reactors at Laguna Verde, Veracruz will likely be fin-
ished in 1983 with a capacity of 2,300 mw.[98] The construction of the light water reactor is expected to begin in
February of 1982. Mexico aims to supply as much as
32 percent of its electricity by nuclear power by the
year 2000.

Foreign trade. By virtue of Mexico's huge quantities of oil reserves and increasing oil production rates,
Mexco's foreign trade will certainly be expanding. As
indicated earlier, over half of Mexico's oil production
is used domestically, the remaining half is exported.

---

[96] World Business Weekly, May 26, 1980, P. 15.

[97] Ibid.

[98] Recuento Nacional, "Sector Energéticos y Petroquímoco", Comercio Exterior, Vol. 31, No. 10, October 1981, P. 1114

The proportions of total foreign trade of various
sectors certainly has changed. Crude petroleum exports
was the leading force growing at very fast rates. Between 1977 and 1981 crude petroleum exports grew by
1585 percent in dollar terms. Only cattle exports were
somewhat similar in this regard growing by 225 percent.
Table 1.11 below gives a year-to-year glimpse of the
main products traded from 1977 to 1980. The traditional
export earners: coffee, cotton, and sugar, have been
crowded out of their leading positions by oil exports.
In the Imports side, Mexico showed an impressive growth
in car spare parts and component imports between 1977
and 1980, with amounted to a 593 percent growth. It was
this rapid growth of car spare parts imports which led
the Mexican government to impose a drastic cut on this
kind of imports by the end of 1981.

Table 1.11
Main Products Traded ($ mn)

	1977	1978	1979	1980
EXPORTS				
Crude Petroleum	890.0	1,663.2	3,754.6	9,429.6
Coffee	454.3	329.4	531.5	415.2
Cotton	77.8	114.1	309.3	320.9
Shrimps	162.0	78.2b	23.1	7.8
Cattle	23.6	81.8	104.5	76.7
Fresh or Frozen meat	45.4	71.9		
Flourspar	39.7	53.3		
IMPORTS	1977	1978a		
Electrical Machinery	415.0	386.4	449.4	1,086.0
Car Spares & Components	356.6	517.0	1,618.5	2,471.8
Maize	191.0	167.8	115.0	589.0
Paper	164.4	76.8	421.5	632.0
Plastic Materials	149.4	200.1	421.5	632.0
Petroleum Products	154.3	195.7	339.6	535.1
Fats & Oils	45.7	83.9	–	–
Cars	6.1	16.3	–	–

Source: Banco de Mexico; Informe Anual 1980, Pags. 177,
184, 191, 200.

Despite impressive crude oil export gains , Mexico's
appetite for imports exceeds its exports. In every year
since 1974 Mexico has had a balance of trade deficit. In
no year since 1974 has the ratio of exports to imports
been higher than 76 percent. Preliminary figures for
1981 indicate that the trade deficit has worsened and
the ratio exports to imports reached almos 83 percent.
Table 1.12 shows this trend in Foreign Trade.

Much of this trade gap is filled by a surplus on in-
visibles coming from earnings on tourism and border
transactions. The remainder of the gap is filled by
over seas borrowing contributing to capital account surplus.

Table 1.12
Trend of Foreign Trade ($ mn)

YEAR	EXPORTS	IMPORTS	BALANCE OF TRADE	EXPORTS AS A % OR IMPORTS
1974	2,850.0	-6,057.0	-3,207.0	47.0
1975	2,869.0	6,580.0	-3,721.0	43.4
1976	3,315.8	6,029.6	-2,713.8	55.0
1977	4,161.5	5,487.5	-1,326.0	75.8
1978	5,437.9	7,560.7	-2,122.8	71.9
1979*	8,577.7	11,916.7	-3,338.9	71.9
1980	15,307.5	18,572.2	-3,264.7	82.4

Sources: 1974 - 1978 Banco de Mexico
          1979 IMF Financial Statistics, April 1980
          Banco de Mexico, Informe Anual 1980.

Mexico's main trading partner is its norther neigh-
bor, the U.S. Japan between 1977 and 1980 made somewhat
significant inroads into the Mexican market by increasing its proportion of total imports from 5.4 percent to 6.0 percent. The U.S. also gained. It was the
most favored country since U.S. exports to Mexico increased from 63.6 percent in 1977 to 68.9 in 1980.
Table 1.13 below gives Mexico's major trading partners
and their proportional share of Mexico's exports and
imports.
    A small proportion of Mexico's trade is with members
of the Latin American Trade Association (Asociacion
Latino Americana de Libre Comercio - ALALC). Part of
the reason for this realatively small proportion of
trade with members of ALALC - Argentina, Brazil, Chile,
Paraguay, Peru and Uruguay - may be due to the failure
of member countries to achieve its alleged goal of
reducing tariffs. As manufacturing plays an increasingly
important role in the economies of member countries, the
clamor for protection remains. The schedule for reducing tariffs to guarantee 'substantially free' trade
was shifted from 1973 to 1980.
    Mexico's foreign trade is robust and with increases
in petroleum production is likely to expand even more.
However, a few dangers loom on the horizon. A policy of
protectionism may permanently disable domestic companies
to effectively compete on world markets. Mexico's rapid

Table 1.13
Main Trading Partners (% of Total)

EXPORTS	1977	1978
USA	58.2	64.0
Brazil	3.6	2.8
West Germany	2.1	2.9
Venezuela	2.1	1.7
Japan	1.9	1.7
Spain	1.3	2.0
Switzerland	1.3	0.8
UK	1.0	0.7
EEC	5.9	5.2
Alalc	8.9	7.3
IMPORTS	1977	1978
USA	63.6	60.4
West Germany	5.7	7.1
Japan	5.4	8.1
Canada	3.0	1.7
France	2.9	3.7
UK	2.3	2.5
Italy	1.9	3.1
Brazil	1.9	1.7
EEC	14.7	18.5
Alalc	4.4	4.0

Source: IMF Direction of Trade; Year Book, 1981,
        Banco de Mexico Annual Report,1981.

pace of oil exploitation might tend to divert resources
from Mexico's traditional exports in agriculture, re-
districting Mexico's export options. Continued large
deficits might have an impact upon the exchange rate of
the Mexican peso, decreasing its buying power in world
markets. If the problems are confronted vigorously and
resolutely, Mexico status as a significant world economic
leader might soon well emerge.

    The financial sector. Mexico has one of the most
developed banking systems of Latin America. The Central
Bank, the Bank of Mexico -founded in 1925-, started
operation in 1932[99]. It has the central responsibility

---

[99] B. Griffiths, Mexican Monetary Poling and Economic Development
(New York: Praeger Publishers, 1972) P. 30

of orchestrating monetary policy:

> ...It decides on the nominal and real levels of
> the rediscount rate, grants rediscounting fa-
> cilities, operates the complicated system of
> reserve requirements imposed on financial
> intermediaries, sets maximum nominal interest
> rates for various deposits and loans, super-
> vises foreign transaction, is the sole issuer
> of paper currency, and regulates the issues of
> certain government bonds. Because reserve re-
> quirements are imposed on nonbank financial
> intermediaries and because the central bank
> fixes the level of nominal rates for these
> institutions, its power vis-a-vis the financial
> sector is greater than it would be in many
> other[100] countries.

The National Financiera is the second most important
official bank. It has been since its establishment in
1932 one of the must important agents in the promotion
of Mexico's industrialization.

The structure of the commercial banking system in
Mexico used to be rather complicated before 1978. It
was integrated by numerous private financial interme-
diaries who were restricted to provide only one kind
of the following financial service.[101] 1) Deposit banks,
2) Savings trust companies, 3) Financieras, 4) Mortgage
credit trust companies, 5) Capitalization companies,
6) Trust companies and 7) Savings and loan banks for
family housing.

The regulation limiting the amount of services provided by a commercial bank was removed in 1978. Commercial banks were allowed to merge and to operate the
seven basic financial services already described. The
merging banks were denominated "Multiple Banking". In
1981 "Multiple Banking" captured 98 percent of the
total financial resources managed by the banking industry in Mexico which amounted to 3483.3 billion Mexican[102]
pesos. In 1979 the commercial banks managed 1566 billion pesos.

The banking industry after the merging process has
shown a high degree of concentration. The two largest
commercial banks -the Bank of Commerce (BANCOMER) and
the National Bank of Mexico (BANAMEX)- controlled

---

[100]Ibid

[101]Ibid

[102]J. López Portillo, "5°Informe de Gobierno", Comercio Exterior,
  Vol. 19, P. 1049.

46 percent of the total Mexican financial resources in 1980. The top management of BANAMEX has publicly expressed concern about the "small size" of the Mexican banks relative to those of the international banking corporation.[103] The national Banking Commission which supervises the operation of the commercial banks seems to have rather different opinion about the bigness of BANAMEX and BANCOMER, since it has somewhat restricted their growth by limiting their opening of new subsidiaries.

Table 1.14 below gives a glimpse of the money and banking situation from 1978 to 1981.

Table 1.14
Money & Banking (End of Quarter bn Pesos)

	1978				
	1Qtr	2Qtr	3Qtr	4Qtr	
Currency in Circulation	84.9	88.6	88.3	115.5	
Demand Deposits:					
deposits & savings banks	102.3	109.1	113.7	142.1	
Advances:					
deposits & savings banks	98.5	116.4	132.8	1,491	
Development banks	486.6	491.2	523.2	532.4	
	1979				
	1Qtr	2Qtr	3Qtr	4Qtr	
Currency in Circulation	105.7e	111.4	118.4	149.6	
Demand Deposits:					
deposits & savings banks	142.6	154.0	153.5	196.6	
Advances:					
deposits & savings banks	133.1	141.6	150.8	180.6	
Development banks	396.0	415.6	439.2	549.3	
	1980				1981
	1Qtr	2Qtr	3Qtr	4Qtr	1Qtr
Currency in Circulation	138.4	145.5	152.5	199.7	212.8
Demand Deposits:					
deposits & savings banks	188.1	193.8	212.1	261.2	266.1
Advances:					
deposits & savings banks	185.9	201.1	227.5	256.6	321.4
Development banks	531.6	561.9	614.9	745.7	830.1

Sources: E.I.U, Quarterly Economic Review of Mexico, 1st quarter 1980, appendix I.
IMF, International Statistics, May 1981.

---

[103] A. Legorreta, Mexico Vision de los Ochenta, P. 176.

During 1980 the money supply increased 32 percent,[104] as a result first of the credits granted by the Banco de Mexico to the federal government[105] to partially finance its deficit and secondly as a result of the non sterilization of foreign assets.[106] International reserves held by el Banco de Mexico in September of 1981 amounted to 10,397[107] million of U.S. Dollars which was 1.66 times the international reserves held by the Central Bank a year earlier, and is also the highest ever held by el Banco de Mexico.[108]

Public Finance. The proportion of GDP given to government consumption has more than doubled in Mexico since 1952 when government outlays were only 4.1 percent of GDP. They were 11.2 percent in 1980. Table 1.15 shows this gradual increase since 1969.

Table 1.15
Government Consumption vs. Proportion of GDP in Mexico

YEAR	GDP	GOV'T CONSUMPTION	PERCENT
1969	374.9	28.8	7.7
1970	418.7	32.6	7.8
1971	452.4	36.7	8.1
1972	512.3	43.7	8.5
1973	619.6	58.1	9.4
1974	813.7	75.7	9.3
1975	988.3	75.8	7.7
1976	1,228.0	105.7	9.4
1977	1,674.7	176.1	10.5
1978	2,104.6	228.4	10.9
1979	2,767.0	317.0	11.5
1980	3,824.0	428.2	11.2

Source: Adapted from IMF International Statistics, April 1976 and May 1981.

[104] J. López Portillo, "5° Informe de Gobierno", Comercio Exterior, P. 1049.
[105] Ibid.
[106] Ibid.
[107] Ibid.
[108] Ibid.

In comparison to other LDC's this proportion is rather small. The relatively small weight of government taxation is best exemplified by the fact that, in the late 1960s, Mexico ranked sixty-sixth of seventy-two countries in terms of the ratio of tax revenues to Gross Domestic Product (GDP).

In the late 1960s taxes and fees accounted for 70 to 75 percent of government revenues, and 'other incomes', largely revenues from so-called decentralized agencies and enterprises with state participation, comprised the rest.

Table 1.16 depicts the sources of Mexico's Federal Government Tax Revenues. From 1970 through 1980 income tax dropped as a mayor component from 58.1 percent of total tax revenue to only 13.3 percent.

Table 1.16
National Budget Revenues (in billion pesos)

	1975	%	1979	%	1980	%
Income Taxes	46.200	13.3	173.0	14.0	246.1	13.0
Tax on Exploitation of Natural Resources	1.925	.6	7.8	0.6	23.5	1.2
Tax on Industry	32,550	9.4	0.	0.	0.	0.
Sales Tax	24.150	7.0	0.	0.	0.	0.
Stamp Tax	1.450	.4	0.	0.	0.	0.
Import Duties	11.726	3.4	28.8	2.3	47.7	2.3
Export Duties	4.400	1.3	34.2	2.7	136.5	7.2
Other Taxes	2.326	.7	74.2	6.0	88.7	4.5
Social Security Quotas	19.954	5.8	82.2	6.6	106.6	5.6
Fees for Public Services	2.620	.8	NA	0.	NA	NA
Proceeds	2.400	.7	NA	0.	NA	NA
Other Non-Tax Income	1.280	.4	15.9	1.3	28.2	1.5
Income from Sale of Goods	.150	.1	NA	0.	NA	NA
Capital Recuperation	.750	.2	1.4	1.3	2.2	0.1
Income from Borrowings	54.181	15.6	237.2	19.2	271.3	14.3
Other Income from: Autonomous Agencies and State Controlled Enterprises	108.2	30.9	319.8	25.9	535.1	28.3
Borrowings of State-Controlled Enterprises	32.306	9.3	172.9	14.0	295.0	15.6
Value Added Tax			83.5	6.8	110.4	5.8
Total Revenues		346.4 100.0	1231.1	100.0	1891.1	100.0

Sources: Kurian P. 993 and
"La Cuenta Pública 1980", Comercio Exterior, Sept., 1981
P. 979, taken from SPP, La Cuenta de la Hacienda Publi-
ca Federal, Vol. 1, Mexico 1980.

Noteworthy too is the significant decline of the importance of both import and export taxes as a source of government revenue. In 1955 these taxes consisted 14.8 percent and 23.5 percent of total tax revenue respectively. By 1980 they comprised only 2.3 percent.

Large leaps tend always to occur in both revenue and expenditure during the last years of a president's term of office. These peaks in government activity are due to efforts by the outgoing incumbent to complete government projects undertaken during his administration.

The government trend in expenditures from 1941 to 1980 has been away from military expenditures to social and debt expenditures. Table 1.16 shows the lack of importance of defense spending in global government expenditures.

Since 1977 the budget has been expansionary. The Mexican government has made full use of PEMEX's revenues to bolster economic development. A major revision which stands out in its revenue sources is the reduction of tax burden on lower income groups by 30 percent. This should help to correct, in part, Mexico's problem of unequal income distribution. PEMEX revenues will no doubt fill in for this foregone revenue from the lower income groups, since PEMEX will pay by 1982 a tax amounting one billion pesos every day. Table 1.17 shows the tremendously large magnitude of budgetry increases from 1975 to 1980.

PEMEX has gotten the largest percentage increase of any single budgetary sector. The budget also reflects Mexico's determined efforts to remove supply bottlenecks by increasing allocation to communications and transportation. Recent problems with agriculture have made it inavoidable that more financial concern be shown for this sector. A mixture of guaranteed prices for farm produce and food subsidies has required a sizeable budgetary increase.

In 1981 the Mexican government increased its expenditure by a rather large amount over 1978 and 1979. The expenditure level was raised from 912 billion pesos in 1978 to 1,891 billion pesos in 1980. This change represented an increase in federal government revenues of 107 percent in a three year period. The largest portion of this budget was slated to go to energy 318 billion (14.3); then debt services, 499 billion pesos (22.4%); health and social security, 291 billion pesos (13%); and agriculture, 145 billion (6.4%).

Public investment is a large and growing sector of government expenditure. A part of total public investment is channeled to the industrial sector via Nacional Financiera. This institution holds a controlling interest over the country's largest steel producer, Altos Hornos de Mexico. It also holds substantial financial

Table 1.17
National Budget Expenditures (in billion pesos)

SECTOR	1975	%	1979	%	1980	%
Agriculture & Livestock	14.3	4.2	79.3	5.6	145.1	6.4
Communication & Transportation	4.3	1.3	66.3	4.7	101.3	4.5
Commerce	0.7	0.2	46.4	3.3	77.8	3.4
Health & Welfare	4.7	1.3	208.9	14.9	291.7	13.0
National Properties	1.2	0.3				
Energy	NA		224.6	16.0	318.1	14.3
Administration	5.3	1.5	46.8	3.3	65.8	2.9
Public works	6.5	1.9	9.6	0.7	16.4	0.07
Defense & Navy	7.6	2.2	15.1	1.0	19.2	0.05
Tourism	0.2	0.05	3.0	0.2	4.5	
Legislature Judiciary & Executive	1.5	0.4	1.2	0.1	1.8	
Regional Development	48.2	13.9	12.5	0.9	26.6	1.1
Public Education	29.0	8.4	NA			
Transfer to Autonomous Agencies & State Controlled Enterprises	139.0	40.1	536.1	38.1	887	39.8
Other	48.7	15.5	153.5	10.9	272	12.2
Total Expenditures	346.5	100.0	1404.0		2227.6	100.0
Public Debt	34.4	9.9	162.0	11.5	499.5	22.4

Source: Kurian, P. 993 and adapted from SPP, La Cuenta de la Hacienda Publica Federal, 1980.

stakes in pulp and paper, fertilizer, electrical equipment, electrohlic copper, sugar, films, textiles, food, beer, chemicals, cement, glass, metal working and hotels.[109]

Official banks are also a conduct through which government investment flows. These banks namely, Banco Nacional de Comercio Exterior, The Banco Nacional de Obras Publicas, The Banco de Fomento Co-operativo, The

---

[109] E.I.U. Annual Supplement 1979, P. 17.

44

Banco Nacional de Credito Rural, and the Sociedad Mexica
na de Credito Industrial.

The announced 1982 budget displays Mexico's determination to keep high its development pace of economic
activity. A large part of this effort will depend upon
a deficit finance approach.

As a general strategy Mexico intends not to finance
development out of current oil revenues, but intends to
borrow funds and finance development expansion using the
oil in the ground as a type of collateral to back-up its
debtor status and use the appreciating flows of future
oil revenues to retire debt.[110]

Inflation

Inflation appears to be almost an intractable problem. The governor of the Banco de Mexico attributed recent high inflation rates to external and structural
problems:

> The sharp increase in world inflation, as well
> as the bottlenecks in sectors such as trans-
> portation, were among the main elements that
> pushed up the domestic rate of inflation,[111]
> bringing it from 16.7% in 1978 to 32% during
> 1981.[111]

But in 1978 the money supply increased by 33.5 percent
and had not abated in its rate on increase during the
year 1980 in which year it grew at a rate of 32 percent.

Continued influxes of money into the economy coupled
with the external and structural problems are assuming
continued high rates of inflation and the subsequent
problems that inflation poses to accurate economic calcu
lation.

Inflation is having extraordinary effects upon those
areas that are close to the developing petroleum areas.
Tabasco is a case in point:

> Fear already has become reality in Tabasco, a
> mostly primitive southeastern state where new
> oil wells gave Mexico much of the 1.6 billion
> dollars it earned in petroleum revenues last
> year (1978). High-paid oil workers have poured
> into the state, straining its limited supply of
> consumer goods and housing. Result: sky-
> rocketing costs.

---

[110]"Mexico: Traying to Use Oil in Place of GATT", World Business
   Weekly, July 7, 1980, P. 21.
[111]Romero Kolbeck G., "The Mexican Economy in the 80s" Euromoney,
   Apnt. 1980.

An apartment in the capital of Villahermosa
that rented for 300 pesos ($15) a month two
years ago now cost 3,000 pesos ($150). Food
prices have doubled. Unskilled Mexicans come
in droves looking for work.
'We here in Villahermosa were always poor',
a local resident complains, 'but we were not
desperate. Now we are surrounded by desperate
people from other states.[112]

The inflation situation may diminish many of the expected gains that Mexico had expected to, and expects to
gain from its program of economic development.

Table 1.18 below provides a comparison of the Mexican and the U.S. rate of inflation.

Table 1.18
Inflation Differential Between Mexico and the U.S.

	1977	1978	1979	1980
Mexico	32.1	18.1	20.7	28.7
U.S.	5.8	7.3	8.5	9.0
Difference	26.3	10.8	12.2	19.7

Source: Wharton-Diemex, "Proyeccion Basica 1981-1990,"
Philadelphia, May 1981, P. 15.

The high rate of inflation in Mexico since 1977 has
had two side effects: first it has created a pressure
for the Mexican peso to devaluate at a faster rate in
term of the U.S. currency. This can be seen from the
change in the purchasing power between the U.S. dollar
and Mexican currency. Secondly, it has worsened the
distribution of income, by favoring the real asset
owners, undermining at the same time wage earners;
specially industrial and agricultural workers.

Pollution

Mexico City suffers from two types of pollution:
noise and air. It has the dubious distinction of being
in 1979, the world's second noisiest city and the third
most polluted. This situation does not seem likely to

---

[112]"The Land of Promise that Awaited Carter", vs News and World
Report, February 19, 1979, P. 22.

46

change since effective efforts will require sacrifices
of economic opportunities in other sectors of the economy that Mexico can ill-afford at this juncture in its
economic development. This seems to be Mexico's position despite the fact that Poza Rica near Mexico City
experienced a near smog disaster in 1950.[113] Mexico
City's high altitude worsens the air dilution factor,
which means less air pollution has a more serious impact then the same amount of air pollution at lower
altitudes. As Mexico's standard of living improves and
incomes rise, it is likely that Mexico will become increasingly concerned with pollution problems. But
until then Mexico's attitude towards pollution might approximate other developing countries perspectives where:

> In their eyes, the Third World's relatively un-
> polluted environments had become resources in
> themselves. 'We have plenty to pollute' roared
> a Latin American delegate at one of the (envi-
> ronmental) conferences 'and we'are going to go
> right on polluting'.[114]

Education. If taken over a long period of time, edu
cation in Mexico has made considerable strides.

> In 1910, just before the onset of the Revolution,
> only 24 percent of the elementary-school-age
> population was attending school. By 1930, the
> figure had gone up to 42 percent, and by 1970,
> to over 80 percent. Census figures suggest that
> illiteracy declined from 76.9 percent in 1910
> to 28.3 percent in 1970; other estimates, using
> a more exacting definition, show less than 40
> percent of the population over nine years of
> age to be functionally literate.
> Yet restricted access to upper levels of mexi-
> can education system (secondary, preparatory,
> and university) has helped perpetuate class
> barriers. In 1926, 3,860 students were enrolled
> in secondary or high school, probably no more
> than 4 or 5 percent of the relevant school age
> population. In 1970, the proportion had risen
> to no more than 20 percent.[115]

[113]D. Miller, Mexico: Country report, Working Paper, University of
   Colorado, Boulder, Co., 1978, P. 82.
[114]Benjamin, Higgins and Jean Downs Economic Development of a
   Small Planet. (N.Y.: W.W. Norton and Company, Inc., 1979, P. 10.
[115]Peter H. Smith, "The Wounds of History", The Wilson Quarterly,
   (Summer 1979, Vol. 3, No. 4, P. 137.
   The Hammond Almanac, 1980, P. 625.

In 1975 there were 52,792 primary and secondary
schools, with a combined enrollment of 14,187,600. In
1976 700,000 were enrolled in higher education. Approxi
mately 20 percent of the 1980 federal budget was spent
on education.

Women are under represented in public school enrollment. In 1980 approximately 48% of primary school
enrollment, 36% of secondary enrollment and 20% of post-
secondary enrollment were girls.

Public education is the basic reponsibility of the
Secretaria de Educacion Publica (SEP). No religious
private schools are supposed to operate in Mexico, however, they do, all private schools must conform to the
will of the state.

There are 42 universities; the largest of which is
the Universidad Nacional Autonoma de Mexico which enrolled 222,982 students of the total nationally enrolled
student population of 514,909 in 1975.[116]

Summary

All the information provided so far, shows that the
recent development of the oil industry in Mexico has
permeated practically all areas of the Mexican economy.
Any modeling of the Mexican economy then, has to be
concerned with the way in which PEMEX, the national oil
company affects the overall economy.

The overall economy on the other hand, can be theoretically approached from different angles. The theoretical paradigm which I have chosen is the one proposed
by the monetary approach to the balance of payments,[117]
having always in mind the importance of the oil sector.

The brief description of the Mexican economy so far
outlined was undertaken: first to identify institutional
variables important enough to be placed in the econometric specifications of the Mexican model which will
be attempted in Chapter 2; second, to provide some
institutional grounds to interpret the econometric results presented at the end of Chapter 3.

---

[116]Kurian, P. 999.

[117]H.G. Johnson and J.A. Frenkel, The Monetary Approach to the
Balance of Payments, George Allen and Unwin, London 1976.

2
The Description of the Model

Since the oil sector is expected to play a critical role in the future evolution of the Mexican economy, the first step we took was to divide the Mexican economy into two sectors: the oil and the non-oil sectors, where causality is expected to run from the oil sector to the non-oil sector, via the effects of oil exports on the money supply.

THE OIL SECTOR

The oil sector, which from now on will be referred to as PEMEX, has certain features which are convenient to describe at this point. First of all, PEMEX is a monopoly legally authorized to operate as such under Mexican law. The monopoly is the only entity legally entitled to extract, refine and distribute oil and oil products. The final distribution of gasoline products is made through a national network of private gasoline station ownership, which in order to be allowed to distribute the product, have to comply with PEMEX regulations.

PEMEX regulates the final price of the product, which cannot be changed by the gas station owners under any circumstances. PEMEX also regulates the schedules for selling gasoline, the amount of gasoline to be sold, the architectural design of the building (in some cases), and the number of pumps allowed to operate in each case.

PEMEX is under the management of a chairman -El Director General de PEMEX- who is appointed by the president, who has the stature of a minister, and who is considered a member of the cabinet.

The chairman of PEMEX is under the direct scrutiny of a board of directors, the president of which is the minister of industrial development -Secretario de Patrimonio y Fomento Industrial-, and is also a member

48

of the board of directors, the president of PEMEX's labor union.

Domestic price policies and oil extraction policies have been set according to general economic development considerations. International price policies have never been openly disclosed, but there seems to be evidence that PEMEX crude oil prices follow within the range of those set by Saudi Arabia who is an important OPEC member.

Oil extraction since the expropriation and until very recently had been mainly dictated by domestic market considerations. Extraction usually grew at the rate of growth of domestic consumption for two reasons: first, because the different administrations after 1938 adopted a cheap energy policy, and secondly, because a lack of international market for Mexican exports which could hardly compete with the cheap and high quality Arab oil. However, the oil embargo and the energy crisis which developed afterwards have encouraged PEMEX's management to adopt a faster rate of extraction and a more aggresive exploration policy. Both policies have paid dividends in terms of PEMEX's total revenues and size of proven reserves. In this general context, the increased amount of crude oil exported has raised the total amount of Mexican exports, and has provided foreign cash to pay for needed imports. The faster rate of oil extraction seems so far to have had a strong impact on the rate of growth of PEMEX's investments. It has had also, as a by-product, a severe impact on the environment which does appear not to have been seriously assessed as yet. This rate of oil extraction on the other hand has required a large amount of investment expenditure, from which an important part is expended on imported capital goods. PEMEX's imports have so far been able to more than offset the effect of crude oil exports on balance of payments. In light of what has been said so far, it can be seen that much of the investment expenditure is on imported capital goods which somehow have lessened the impact of oil exports on the balance of payments current account.

Accordingly, PEMEX's[1] total revenues (TR) have two sources: the domestic sales of all oil products (Rd), plus crude oil exports (Rf), usually priced in terms of United States dollars. That is,

1) $TR = Rd + Rf$

---

[1] The mathematical development of PEMEX, the Mexican oil company, is thoroughly described in the mathematical appendix.

These revenues usually have two uses: to cover the total cost of production and to pay taxes. Sometimes there must be some revenue left for PEMEX with no specific use. However, for purposes of analysis it will be assumed that total net revenues for PEMEX are always zero. That is,

$$NR = \{Pd \ (1-n) \ [Qd \ (y)] \ - \ Cd\} \ +$$

$$+ \ \{Px \ (1-m) \ [Qx \ (Px, \ \frac{1}{y} \ \frac{dy}{dt}, \ Rp \ (T,G) \ - \ Cf] \ +$$

$$+ \ S \ = \ 0$$

where NR is total net revenue of PEMEX, the term within the first brackets is net revenue of domestic sales after taxes, the term within the second bracket is net revenue on crude oil exports, Pd is the weighted average price of oil products sold domestically, Qd a function of the level of national income (Y), is the amount of oil products sold domestically, Cd is the cost of production of domestic sales, n and m are the proportion of taxes levied on domestic and foreign PEMEX's sales, Px, Qx and Cf are the price, quantity and cost of production of oil exports respectively, and S is the government subsidy to PEMEX. Qx on the other hand, is assumed to be a function of the world price of crude oil exports (Px), the rate of change of national income ($\frac{1}{Y} \ \frac{dY}{dt}$) and the amount of proven reserves (Rp) which are also a function of the current technology usted to test the existence of oil resources (T) and the amount of resources allocated for exploration research purposes (G). If we recall that it was said earlier that PEMEX is a government owned and controlled corporation the domestic or export prices of which very often are set up according to goals different from profit maximization, then it can be seen that it has been possible for the oil company in the recent past to report losses[2] in some years. Since government price policies are sometimes the real reason behind "red numbers", especially in domestically sold products, the government steps up and subsidizes the deficit (S) by returning part of the collected taxes. However, if the subsidy

---

[2] S.P.P., La Industria Petrolera en Mexico, Mexico 1980, p.401.

is above the amount of taxes received, the government will probably revert either to the general fund or will act as a guarantor on loans to cover the deficit. Since losses most likely occur on domestic sales, we will assume that all the deficit is part of PEMEX's revenues. Equation (2) may then be re-expressed as follows":[3]

(3) $NR = \{Pd(1 - n)\ Qd(Y) + S - Cd\} +$

$\{Px(1 - m)\ [Qx(Px, \frac{1}{y}\ \frac{dy}{dt}, R_P(T\ G))] - C_f\} = 0$

where subsidies (S) has been incorporated as a PEMEX domestic revenue. Now we are ready to analyze how PEMEX may affect the rest of the economy through its effect on monetary variables. If we take the net domestic revenue after taxes -first bracket-, the net revenue on domestic sales after taxes has to be at least equal to zero, since if any losses are reported, these will be covered by means of a subsidy (S); hence,

(4) $Cd = \{Pd(1 - n)\ Qd(Y)\}\ +\ S$

The specification in (4) suggest that if domestic net revenues -the expression within brackets on the right side of 4- are equal to the total cost of domestic goods sold, (Cd) then the subsidy (S) will be zero. However, if the cost of goods sold domestically (Cd) is above PEMEX's domestic net revenue after taxes, then the subsidy (S) will be greater than zero, which implies that government revenues will be less than expected. If it is further assumed, let us say, that the only possible way to finance PEMEX's deficit by the government is by borrowing from the central bank -El Banco de Mexico-. then the oil sector is affecting via government financing, the level of money supply[4] which will produce a chain of events that I will label as the subsidy effect. If we

---

[3] There is no reason to differentiate the cost of domestic oil products sold domestically, and those sold on the world market within equation (3), except for identification purposes, where we have Cd, the cost of domestic products, and C_f the cost of export products.

[4] The subsidy effect may be produced by any government owned company and not only by PEMEX. Hence our interest will not center around this mechanism.

take into consideration now the expression within the
second bracket, which is PEMEX's net revenue on crude
oil exports, -assumed to be greater than or equal to
zero- posted in terms of the taxes, we have that PEMEX's
paid taxes on crude oil exports -the left hand side expression in equation (5) - are equal to PEMEX's net revenues $(R_f - C_f)$ on crude oil exports.

$$(5) \quad mPx \quad Qx(Px, \frac{1}{y} \frac{dy}{dt}, R_p (G, T)) \quad = \quad R_f - C_f$$

Analyzing the expression in (5) we find no reason for
PEMEX to export at a loss on the margin, considering
taxes as a cost which PEMEX has to pay to the nation as
a fee for the right to exploit non-renewable resources
in order to serve a foreign market.

Hence it seems reasonable to expect that the amount
of taxes collected on crude oil exports -the left hand
side expression of equation (5)- will be at least equal
to those expected by the government. As taxes on crude
oil exports are assumed to be a fixed proportion of the
foreign revenue of PEMEX, the government can collect
them directly in terms of a hard foreign currency
(dollars, yens, sterling pounds) and use them either to
finance government expenditures or to pay part of the
domestic or foreign public debt. If government revenues
on crude oil exports are used to finance public expenditures on foreign goods (corn, wheat and milk for the
poor, the children and the elderly) the net effect of
PEMEX exports on current account of the balance of
payments will be partially neutralized. If the government revenues are spent on domestic goods the net effect
of PEMEX exports on current account will be fully reflected as a change in the monetary base. If government revenues on PEMEX's crude oil exports are allocated
to pay part of the public debt to the central bank, then
the net effect of PEMEX's crude oil exports will be
sterilized and will have no impact on domestic variables.
If government revenues on PEMEX's crude foreign sales is
allocated to pay part of the foreign public debt, then
the net effect of PEMEX revenues on current account
will be partially neutralized.

All the alternatives presented, arising out of
PEMEX's crude oil exports are the important ones for our
purposes, given their implications on Balance of
Payments current account, on monetary variables, and the
further impact of monetary variables on the rest of the
economic system. The subsidy granted by the government
to PEMEX domestic sales and its further impact on monetary variables, the subsidy effect, is not of our concern and will be left out, since the "subsidy effect"
can be produced by any government owned company, and

not only by PEMEX. Whereas, a serious effect on Balance
of Payments current accounts certainly can only be
brought about by PEMEX and no other private or public
corporation given the current economic conditions of the
country.

THE TRANSMISSION MECHANISM

For the moment, let us assume that the overall balance of payments is equal to the current account balance. Let us further assume that PEMEX's foreign revenues are of a magnitude such that they are able to
produce a current account balance surplus. Since for
the moment the result in current account is identical
to the result in overall balance of payments, then the
surplus is equally identical to the changes in net foreign assets held by the central bank, and then we expect the surplus produced by the oil exports to increase the amount of foreign assets held by El Banco
de Mexico. Since the monetary base is identical to the
amount of net and foreign assets held by the central
bank, then if the net foreign assets increase, the
monetary base will also increase by the same amount.
The money supply is regarded as equal to the monetary
base times the money multiplier, and an increase in the
base will increase the money supply. There exists a
desired amount in cash balances that the public wishes
to hold, and for the purposes of analysis, let us assume
that this stock of desired real cash balances is equal
to the amount of real stock money supplied before the
surplus in the balance of payments occurred. Then the
balance of payments surplus will produce an excess of
stock money supply. The public is expected to react to
the excess of stock cash balances by exchanging their
excess of cash balances for domestic and foreign bonds
and goods and services. If there is some level of
unemployed resources, then we expect the excess of
demand for domestic goods with a lag to be partially
reflected in increase in the price of domestic goods.
Another "escape valve" is the foreign market. The
excess of demand for foreign goods is expected to affect
the level of imports and hence the level of the balance
of payments surplus. This chain of events is expected
to go on until the surplus becomes zero. A more complex
mechanism of variation will be tried in the proposed
model, which will have a more complex balance of
payments block than the one described here, and a fully
developed money market. However, what we have attempted
to do here was to point out the several channels
through which the oil sector may affect the non-oil
sector of the Mexican economy.

THE STRUCTURE OF THE NON-OIL SYSTEM

The workings of the non-oil sector or, more con-
veniently, "the rest of the economy," is described in
Figure 2. Before starting its description, it must be
made clear that from now on the oil sector will be
treated esentially as exogenous to the "rest of the
economy" subsystem, and that the modelling process
will be concerned with the analysis of the behavior of
the non-oil sector. Economic causation is expected
to run from the oil sector to the rest of the economy
via balance of payments and money supply, in a fashion
already described.
To begin with, we will assume that in equilibrium
aggregate demand (Qd) equals aggregate supply (Qs),
that is,

(6)   Qd = Qs

Substracting from both sides of (6), the ex-ante
aggregate supply and demand in equilibrium of the oil
sector, we have as a residual the corresponding aggregate of the non-oil sector. That is,

(7)   Ys = Yd

where Ys is the aggregate supply and Yd aggregate demand. On the demand side, we know that in this economy
expenditures can be made by households, in which case
they are called "consumption" (C), by firms, in which
case they are called "investment"[5] (I), or by the
government, in which case they are called "government
expenditures" (G). Also, households, firms, and the
government in order to achieve their market transactions, require the intermediation of money. Each
individual believes himself to be able to add to or
substract from his actual cash holdings at current
prices by spending less or more than his income. If
he decides to spend less than his income he is in the
process of hoarding. If he decides to spend more than
his income he is regarded as being in the process of
dishoarding. The decisions of all individuals to hoard
or dishoard may cause aggregate expenditures to be
different from aggregate income. Hence equation (7)
can be re-expressed as follows:

---

[5]Includes changes in inventories.

55

THE STRUCTURE OF THE MEXICAN SYSTEM

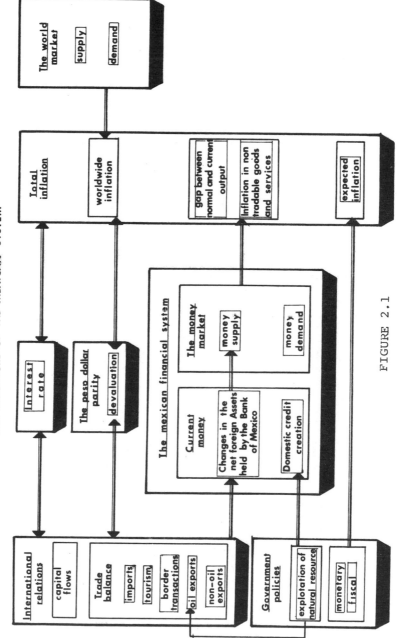

FIGURE 2.1

(8) $Y_{s_t} = C_t + I_t + G_t + D_t$

where Y_{s_t}, C_t, I_t and G_t are as defined before, and D_t the nominal flow demand for cash balances.

Equation (8) can also be re-expressed in real terms without any loss of generality as follows:[6]

(9) $(\dfrac{Y}{p})_t = (\dfrac{C + I + G}{p})_t + (\dfrac{D}{p})t$

Equation (9) could also be re-expressed as follows:

(10) $(\dfrac{Y}{P})_t = (\dfrac{GA}{P})_t + (\dfrac{D}{P})_t$

where the first term on the right side, (GA/p), is real aggregate expenditure[7] of the non-oil sector and the second $(D/p)_t$ may be termed real hoarding.[8]

We know that for any country engaged in international trade, as Mexico is, the aggregate demand has a foreign component the importance of which depends upon the degree of openness of the economy. To consider the foreign components of the aggregate demand $(Yd)_t$: equation (9) can also be expressed[9] as

(11) $(\dfrac{Y}{P})_t = (\dfrac{C + I + G}{P})_t + (\dfrac{X}{PX} - \dfrac{M}{PM})_t$

where $(\dfrac{X}{PX})_t$ are ex-ante real exports of the non-oil sector and $(\dfrac{M}{PM})_t$ are ex-ante real imports of the non-oil sector.

---

[6] For further details, see R. Dornsbusch, "Currency Depreciation, Hoarding and Relative Prices," _Journal_ _of_ _Political_ _Economy_, July-August 1973.

[7] S. Alexander, "Effects of Devaluation on the Trade Balance," _IMF_ _Staff_ _Papers_, April 1952, _II_, 263-278

[8] Ibid.

[9] Note that real hoarding, $(D/P)_t$ then equal to the net result in trade balance, $(X/PX-M/PM)_t$.

Since Mexico's main trade partner is the United States,[10] it seems reasonable to assume that the price level of Mexican imports (PM) and exports (PX) will behave in the same fashion as those of the United States' general level (PM), or even more so. We can assume that the price level of exports is equal to the price level of imports, and both of them are equal to the United States' price level, that is,

(12)   PX = PM

Using (11) and (12) in (10), we can re-express aggregate supply as follows:

$$(13) \qquad (\frac{Y}{p})_t \;=\; (\frac{GA}{p})_t \;+\; (\frac{X-M}{PM})_t$$

What we have had so far from (6) through (13) have been identities. To focus upon the identity in (13) as a behavioral equation we will undertake one further step and we will assume that Mexico is a small country which will imply that the "non-oil sector" will have to be a price taker for its imports and exports, that it will have to face an infinitely elastic demand function for its exports, and that the import and export prices will be given, and finally that the level of exports will be exogenously determined, or purely a function of time, that is,

(14)   PX = PM   and

(15)   X = f(t)

Remaining variables to be dealt with are ex-ante real aggregate expenditures $(GA/p)_t$ and the ex-ante real demand for imports $(M/PM)_t$.

REAL DEMAND FOR IMPORTS

The ex-ante demand function of any good as it is usually presented in standard textbooks, is a multivariate function of the price of the own good, (PM), the weighted average price of other goods (P) and money income (Y). This type of specificity applied to the demand for imports would yield the following function:

$$(16) \qquad \frac{P}{PM}\, M \;=\; M\,(PM,\ P,\ Y)$$

---

[10] More than 70 percent of Mexico's total exports and imports are with the United States.

This function is also usually regarded as homogeneous of degree zero in the price of the own good, the weighted price of other goods and income;[11] a property that is used to collapse the demand as a function of only two variables; the relative price of the own good (PM/P) and real income $(\frac{Y}{P})$ or general command over goods and services, that is,

$$(17) \quad \frac{1}{PM} \ M = m \ (\frac{PM}{P} , \frac{Y}{P})$$

However, the kind of specification in (16) has been found unsuitable[12] to deal with the complexities arising out of relations which govern demand conditions in international trade[13] primarily because demand analysis as presented in (17) is used to analyze relations among parts of the economic system.[14]

Alternative specifications for the demand for imports are to exclude income from the argument and, rather, relate imports to aggregate expenditures in the following fashion.

$$(18) \quad \frac{P}{MP} \ M = M \ (PM, P, GA)$$

Also resorting to the homogeneity property again, we can express imports in the real terms as follows:

$$(19) \quad \frac{M}{PM} = m \ (\frac{PM}{P} , \frac{GA}{P})$$

The reasoning behind the formulation in (19) is that in this kind of formulation the domestic demand for foreign goods $(\frac{M}{PM})$ is properly related to domestic

---

[11] M. Friedman, Price Theory, University of Chicago Press, 1976 p. 22.

[12] Alexander, p. 264.

[13] A. Laffer, "The anti-Traditional General Equilibrium Theory of the Rate of Growth and the Balance of Payments Under Fixed Exchange Rate," unpublished, 1978. Also see R. Mundell, Monetary Theory, Good Year, Palisades, California, 1971.

[14] Friedman, p. 29.

demand for foreign goods $(\frac{GA}{P})$,[15] rather than to domestic demand for domestic goods plus foreign demand for domestic goods involved in the specification in (17). More explicitly the ex-ante domestic demand for foreign goods can be expressed in real terms as

$$(20) \quad \frac{M}{PM} = \beta_0 + \beta_1 \left(\frac{PM}{P}\right) + \beta_2 \left(\frac{GA}{P}\right) + U_{1t}$$

where M is the nominal value of imports, PM is the price of imports, P is the domestic price level, and GA is nominal ex-ante aggregate expenditures. U_{1t} is the random variable error term with the classical properties $U_t \sim N(0, \sigma^2_U)$. β_1 and β_2 are the parameters to be estimated, and according to economic theory,[16] they are expected to have the following signs: $\beta_1 < 0$, $\beta_2 > 0$.

Real Aggregate Expenditure

In any basic Keynesian macroeconomic model expenditures are regarded as being made by households (consumption) by firms (investment), and by the government (government expenditures). Real ex-ante consumption[17] $(\frac{C}{P})$ is usually thought of as being an increasing function of real income[18]. It is also postulated that the marginal propensity to consume is less than one. Ex-ante real investment $(\frac{I}{P})$ is thought of as being negatively related to the rate of interest, while real ex-ante government expenditure $(\frac{G}{P})$ is treated exogenously, that is, a variable that may affect, but is not affected by the other variables of the system. This means that real aggregate expenditures $(\frac{GA}{P})$ are a function of real income $(\frac{Y}{P})$ and the interest rate (R mex). If the interest rate goes up, a downward movement along the investment function will take place and expenditures will decrease. If real income increases, un upward movement along the consumption function will take place, and real aggregate expenditure will be raised, that is,

---

[15] M. Khan, "A Monetary Model of Balance of Payments," _Journal of Monetary Economics_, 1976, 2, 313.

[16] A. Kuotsoyiannis, _Modern Microeconomics_, New York 1970, p. 53.

[17] W. L. Smith, "A Graphical Exposition of the Complete Keynesian System," _Southern Economic Journal_, October 1956, _23_, 115-125.

[18] Usually a function of disposable income.

(21) $\qquad (\frac{GA}{P})_t = g \quad (\frac{Y}{P}), R \text{ mex})$

where $\qquad g_1 > 0$

$\qquad\qquad g_2 < 0$

In our approach to modelling, we are taking a some-what different stand. First of all we will take real aggregate expenditure $(\frac{GA}{P})$ in (10) to the right side of the equation as follows:

(22) $\qquad (\frac{GA}{P})_t = (\frac{Y}{P})_t - (\frac{D}{P})_t$

Equation (22) is defining ex-ante real expenditures. $(\frac{GA}{P})_t$ as being equal to ex-ante real income minus desired real hoarding $(\frac{D}{P})_t$. Desired real hoarding is thought of as being the level of the flow demand for real money balances through time. To transform (22) into a behavioral equation, the flow level of real cash balances $(\frac{D}{P})_t$, will be assumed to be a proportional function of the stock excess demand for real money ba-lances, that is,

(23) $\qquad (\frac{D}{Pt}) = \mu[(\frac{M*d}{P})_t - (\frac{Ms}{P})_t]$

where μ, the coefficient of adjustment, is expected to lie between zero and one. $(M*d/P)_t$ is the desired amount of real cash balances in period t, and $(M_s/P)_t$ is the stock of real money balances in year t.

In order to derive the flow demand for real money $(\frac{D}{P})_t$, we have to have some ideas of the specific shape of the function for the desired stock demand for real money.

The Demand for Real Cash Balances

The central subject around which monetary analysis has built up is the demand for money. Similar specifi-cations with different implications have been discussed. From among all the broad possibilities in money demand theories, we have chosen, for the purposes of this paper, an extension of the Cambridge Cash Balance approach. For Cambridge economists such as Marshall, Keynes and Pigou, the demand for money is assumed to be a function of the wealth of the society,[19] the oppor-

---

[19] A.C. Pigou, "The Value of Money", Quarterly Journal of Economics, November 1917, 132, 38-65.

tunity cost of holding money, represented by the pro-
gressive loss of income as a consequence of having
stored the money, which is represented by the interest
rate, and of the expectations with regard to the future
behavior of the price level. The function is assumed
to be of degree one in price and wealth. The assumption
that is used to collapse the real demand for money as a
function of only two variables: the real stock of wealth
(W/P) and the interest rate (R mex). That is,

(24) $\quad \dfrac{M*d}{P} = md \quad (\dfrac{W}{P}, \; R \; mex)$

where $(\dfrac{W}{P})$ is the stock of real wealth, and (R mex) is
the opportunity cost of holding money. For the purpose
of this model, we will adopt a modified version of (24)
by using real income (Y/P), a proxy for the stock of
real wealth $(\dfrac{W}{P})$, as an argument of the function. The
opportunity cost of holding money represented by the
interest rate (R mex) is eliminated as an argument of
the desired demand for money since the short term interest rate in Mexico has been controlled for the
government and it has not been allowed to fluctuate
according to the market forces. Then the officially
recorded interest rate did not usually represent the
market interest rate consistent with the true cost of
holding money in Mexico. For that reason we express
the real stock of money demand more simply as a function
of real income $(Y/P)_t$ as follows:

(25) $\quad (\dfrac{M*D}{P})_t = k(\dfrac{Y}{P})^{\eta} \; ; \; 0 < k < 1 \quad \eta \simeq 1$

where (Y/P) is real income, k is a constant which
measures the proportion of income held in cash balances,
and η is the income elasticity of real cash balances,
which is assumed to be about equal to one. It is
assumed that real income and the real demand for money
will move in the same direction.

Equation (25) explains a long run desired stock of
money balances which may not be satisfied at every point
in time.

Now we are ready to derive the flow demand for real
cash balances by substituing equation (25) into (23) and
solving by the flow demand for real cash balances $(\dfrac{D}{P})_t$.

(26) $\quad (\dfrac{D}{P})_t = \mu \; k(\dfrac{Y}{P}) - \mu(\dfrac{M_s}{P})_t$

Equation (26) is the flow demand for real cash balances, which is different from the real stock demand
for real cash balances specified in (25). This specification will be the cornerstone upon which most of the

later specifications of the model will rely.

With the specification in (26) we are now ready to derive a testable equation for the demand for real aggregate expenditures. Substituting the flow demand for real cash balance (26) in (21), we now have the following specifications for real aggregate expenditures $(\frac{GA}{P})$ that is,

$$(27) \qquad (\frac{GA}{P})_t = (1 - \mu k)(\frac{Y}{P})_t + \mu(\frac{M_s}{P})_t$$

The specification in (27) simply says that real aggregate expenditures in the Mexican economy are a function of the excess of real money supply represented by the flow demand for money, since if the real stock of money is equal to the stock demand for money (Equation 21) then the flow demand for money is zero; otherwise it will be different from zero and will affect the level of real aggregate expenditures through people's adjustments of desired cash balances.

An interesting feature for purposes of estimation is that whereas real aggregate expenditure is a linear function in specifications, it is not in the parameters. We can re-specify (26) in a simpler fashion as follows:

$$(28) \qquad (\frac{GA}{P}) = \beta_7 + \beta_8 (\frac{Y}{P}) + \beta_9 (\frac{M_s}{P})_t + U_{2t}$$

since $0 \leq \mu \leq 1$, then

$$\beta_8 > 0, \ \beta_9 > 0, \ U_{2t} \simeq N(0, \sigma^2 U_{2t})$$

Private Consumption

As we pointed out earlier, Aggregate absorption has several components. The most important of these is private consumption expenditures. Consumption has been a fertile land in which empirical analisis has flourished. A vast literature has been writen on the matter, and there is now a wide consensus that consumption is a positive function of real income or wealth. In this paper I will instead take a view of consumption which will yield basically the same conclusion, from a different theoretical framework which will allow us to incorporate the expected rate of inflation as an explanatory variable of real private consumption.

Desired real private consumption $(\frac{C}{P})^*_t$ is assumed to be a function of the level of aggregate expenditures in period t $(\frac{GA}{P})_t$ and the expected rate of inflation (Π^e_t), that is

(29) $\quad (\frac{C}{P})^{*}_{t} = P(\frac{GA}{P})_{t} + d_0 \; \Pi^{e}_{t}$

where p is the desired proportion of real private consumption among all expenditures, and do is the parameter
which measures the influence of the expected rate of
inflation in the level of real desired expenditures.

It is also assumed that the dynamic adjustment of
current real private consumption $d(\frac{C}{P})_{t}$ is performed
according to the following scheme:

(30) $\quad d(\frac{C}{P})_{t} = q \, [\, (\frac{C}{P})^{*}_{t} - (\frac{C}{P})_{t-1}]$

where d in a difference operator, $(\frac{C}{P})_{t}$ is real private
consumption in period t and $(\frac{C}{P})^{*}_{t}$ is real desired private
consumption in period t, and q is the parameter which
measures the degree of adjustment of desired real private consumption in period t in light of the realized
private consumption in the previous period $(\frac{C}{P})_{t-1}$. Substituting (27) into (29) and (29) into (30) and solving for
$(\frac{C}{P})_{t}$, we have

(31) $\quad (\frac{C}{P})_{t} = qp(1-\mu k) \, (\frac{Y}{P})_{t} + qp\mu \, (\frac{Ms}{P}) + d_0 \; \Pi^{e}_{t} +$

$\quad\quad + (1-q) \; (\frac{C}{P})_{t\,1}$

which is the behavioral equation for real private consumption. If we assume

$\quad\quad c_1 = qP(1 - k\mu)$

$\quad\quad c_2 = qP\mu$

$\quad\quad c_3 = d_0$

$\quad\quad c_4 = (1 - q)$

then we have

(32) $\quad (\frac{C}{P})_{t} = c_0 + c_1 \, (\frac{Y}{P})_{t} + c_2(\frac{Ms}{P}) + c_3 \; \Pi^{e}_{t} +$

$\quad\quad + c_4 (\frac{C}{P})_{t-1} + U_{3t}$

c_1 is the marginal propensity to consume out of real
income, c_2 is the marginal propensity to consume out
of real money, and c_3 is the marginal propensity to
consume out of an expected change in the expected rate
of inflation (Π^{e}_{t}). Since $0 < q, P, k, \mu, < 1$, and

$d_0 < 0$, then the expected signs of the parameters to be estimated are the following: $c_1 > 0$, $c_2 > 0$, $c_3 < 0$, $c_4 > 0$. An interesting feature of consumption in Equation (30) is that real money is included as an explanatory variable, and the desired to hold cash balance which is expected to depress consumption is made explicit as an explanatory component of the marginal propensity to consume out of income in the parameter c_1.

Real Government Expenditures

Desired real government expenditures $(\frac{G}{P})_t^*$ are assumed to be a function of real aggregate absorption $(\frac{GA}{P})$ and some institutional factors (IF). That is,

$$(33) \quad (\frac{G}{P})_t^* = \eta (\frac{GA}{P}) + g \ IF + g_0$$

It is well known that total government revenues in Mexico have four basic uses: the first is to cover the government's overhead represented by wages, salaries, maintenance of buildings, office equipment and so on. A second use is to cover investment in social infrastructure and investment for general purposes of economic development. A third use is to cover the subsidies granted to some economic activities such as the development of "the infant industry" and so on, and also to cover the subsidy granted to the consumption of goods basic in the consumption of low level income households. In this block we are interested only in dealing with the first and third uses of government revenues, which we have classified as government expenditures. To capture the essence of government expenditures, we originally linked it to the result in current account in balance of payments as a proxy variable for subsidies, which is, we believe, the most dynamic element in government expenditures. However, more careful consideration will show that in any event, causality would run from government expenditures in the form of subsidies, to imports, and hence, we decided not to include it in order to avoid a possible misspecification. We rather decided to take the view that government expenditures adjust dynamically to a level of expenditures consequent with a certain level of economic development measured by the level of aggregate absorption, where the higher the level of aggregate absorption, the higher the level of real government expenditures. The dynamic adjustment of aggregate expenditures is assumed to be described by the following expression:

$$(34) \quad d(\frac{G}{P})_t = g \ [(\frac{G}{P})_t^* - (\frac{G}{P})_{t-1}]$$

where d is a difference operator, $(\frac{G}{P})_t^*$ is the desired level of real government expenditures in period t, and $(\frac{G}{P})_t$ is the current level of real government expenditures, g is the parameter which measures the degree of adjustment of desired real government expenditures in light of realized real government expenditures in the previous period, and is assumed to lie between 0 and 1.

Substituting (27) into equation (33) and (33) into (34), and developing the expression, we have:

(35) $(\frac{G}{P})_t = gP(1 - \mu k) \ (\frac{Y}{P})_t + gP\mu \ (\frac{M_S}{P})_t + (1 - g)$

$(\frac{G}{P})_{t-1} + g_0 + U_{4t}$

if we assume

$$g_1 = gP(1 - \mu k)$$

$$g_2 = gP\mu$$

$$g_4 = (1 - g)$$

then we have:

(36) $(\frac{G}{P})_t = g_0 + g_1 (\frac{Y}{P})_t + g_2 (\frac{M_S}{P})_t + g_3 (\frac{G}{P})_{t-1} + U_{4t}$

since $0 < g, p, \mu, k < 1$, and $g_1 < 0$, then the expected signs for the parameters to be estimated are as follows:

$$g_1 < 0, \ g_2 > 0, \ g_3 > 0, \ g_4 > 0$$

Real Private Investment

Real private investment $(\frac{I}{P})_t$ is assumed to depend on the dynamic adjustment of the desired level of capital stock by entrepreneurs. That is:

(37) $(\frac{I}{P})_t = h^\lambda \ [K_t^d - K_{t-1}^d]$

where h is a parameter which measures the adjustment in the desired level of capital stock by entrepreneurs (K_t^*) and λ is the time horizon that entrepreneurs take into consideration during the adjustment process. In our case we assume the entrepreneurs have a very short time horizon to take into consideration, since λ the size of the lag is one period, hence $\lambda = 0, 1$. This specification implies that entrepreneurs are amnesic beyond period one, of course more complex specification can be made simply by extending the time horizon beyond one.

In equation (37) we have real investment $(\frac{I}{P})_t$ as a function of two unobservable variables which are the desired capital stock in the current period $(K^d)_t$ and the period before. In order to posit the equation in terms of observable variables, it is assumed that the desired stock of capital $(K^d)_t$ in any period is a function of the past performance of the economy, measured by the level of aggregate absorption in the previous period, that is,

$$(38) \quad K^d_t = \alpha(\frac{GA}{P})_{t-1}$$

Substituting (27) into (38) and (38) into (37) and developing the expression, we have:

$$(39) \quad (\frac{I}{P})_t = \alpha(1 - \mu k)\ (\frac{Y}{P})_{t-1} - \alpha\ g(1 - \mu\ k)$$

$$(\frac{Y}{P})_{t-2} + \alpha\mu\ (\frac{Ms}{P})_{t-1} - \alpha\ g(1 - \mu k)\ (\frac{Y}{P})_{t-2} +$$

$$+ U_{5t}$$

If we assume

$$i_1 = \alpha(1 - \mu k)$$

$$i_2 = \alpha g(1 - \mu k)$$

$$i_3 = \alpha\mu$$

$$i_4 = \alpha g(1 - \mu k);\quad \text{then we have}$$

$$(40) \quad (\frac{I}{P})_t = i_0 + i_1(\frac{Y}{P})_{t-1} + i_2(\frac{Y}{P})_{t-2} + i_3(\frac{Ms}{P})_{t-1} +$$

$$+ i_4(\frac{Ms}{P})_{t-2} + U_{5t}$$

Since $0 < \alpha,\ \mu,\ k,\ g < 1$, the expected signs of the parameters to be estimated are as follows:

$$i_1 > 0,\ i_2 < 0,\ i_3 > 0,\ i_4 < 0$$

An interesting feature of real private investment in equation (39) is that it does not depend on the opportunity cost of holding money (R_{mex}) as it is usually presented, but rather depends on the level of real money supply $(\frac{Ms}{P})$ and real income $(\frac{Y}{P})$. Also interesting to notice is that the marginal propensity to invest depends on the level of real money supply $(\frac{Ms}{P})$ and real income ($\frac{Y}{P}$). Also interesting to notice is that the marginal propensity to invest depends upon the desired level of hoarding money by the public, which is made an explicit component of the marginal propensity to invest. The higher the desired level of hoarding cash balances, represented by k, the lower the marginal propensity to invest. Hence the desire to hold money is expected to depress investment.

Real Government Investment

In order to produce economic development the government has to invest in a "social capital good" able to produce economic development. Real government investment ($\frac{GI}{P}$) then is assumed to depend on the dynamic adjustment of the desired level of "social capital stock" (K_t^g), that is

(41) $(\frac{GI}{P})_t = h^{\lambda} [K_t^g - K_{t-1}^g]$

where h^{λ} is the parameter which measures the adjustment of government "desired social capital stock" to produce economic development.

In equation (41) we have real government investment ($\frac{GI}{P}$) as a function of an unobservable variable which is "desired social capital stock". In order to posit the equation in terms of observable variable it is assumed that the desired "social capital stock", in any period is a function of the level of real aggregate expenditures ($\frac{GA}{P}$), that is

(42) $K_t^g = \alpha \ (\frac{GA}{P})_{t-1}$

substituting (28) into (42) and (42) into (41) and developing the expression, we have:

(43) $(\frac{GI}{P})_t = \alpha \ (1 - \mu k) (\frac{Y}{P})_{t-1} - \alpha g (1- \ k) (\frac{Y}{P})_{t-2} +$

         $+ \ \alpha\mu \ (\frac{Ms}{P})_{t-1} - \alpha g (1 - \ k) (\frac{Y}{P})_{t-2} + U_{6t}$

If we assume

         $g_1 = \alpha (1 - \mu k)$
         $g_2 = \alpha g (1 - \mu k)$
         $g_3 = \alpha\mu$
         $g_4 = \alpha g (1 - \mu k);$ then we have

$$(44) \quad (\tfrac{GI}{P})_t = g_0 + g_1 (\tfrac{Y}{P})_{t-1} + g_2 (\tfrac{Y}{P})_{t-2} +$$

$$+ g_3 (\tfrac{Ms}{P})_{t-1} + g_4 (\tfrac{Ms}{P})_{t-2} + U_{6t}$$

since $0 < \alpha, \mu, k, g < 1$, the expected signs of the parameter to be estimated are as follows:

$$g_1 > 0, \ g_2 < 0, \ g_3 > 0, \ g_4 < 0$$

The Money Supply

Generally speaking, the sources of the money supply are three. The first source is the currence issued by the central bank (H_t), which is the legal tender of the country. The second source of the money supply is the amount of foreign currency left over as a product of the net result in the overall balance of payments, which, channeled through the domestic banking system, is transformed into domestic currency.[20] It is this element which makes the supply of money an endogenous variable, not subject to the government's control. A third source of money supply is the "private" money created by the domestic banking system, where the banking system is fed with government-issued money. Since the foreign currency is transferred into domestic currency, the two will embrace.

Once the government money is issued, the public in accordance with its scale of preference, will keep part of its holding in this form, and the remaining part may be used to "buy" in cash "private" or "banking" money. The private bank which is "selling" its product -a deposit- to the public in cash will immediately face a state of excess liquidity. If there were no government control over the private banking system, the banks would probably continue selling deposits in cash or in credit indefinitely in order to get rid of the excess liquidity, having as a check only the public desire

---

[20] This statement is not absolutely true, since in Mexico there already exist banking deposits specified in foreign currencies, usually United States dollars. However, for our purposes we will not regard these types of deposits as part of the domestic money supply. This phenomenon is a very interesting one which deserves careful analysis, but which is beyond the scope of this paper.

to hold money in cash or in the form of deposits. However, the private banks are controlled by the central
bank, which in order to guarantee the public's right to
"resale" their deposits to the private banks whenever
they wish, has imposed a reserve requirement -encaje le-
gal- on every peso deposit issued by the private bank.
The required deposit is a portion of every peso deposit
created by the private bank, which has to be deposited
free of interest in the central bank -El Banco de Mexi-
co-. Obviously the imposition of the required reserve
sets a lower limit to the money creation by the private
banking system. It is not to be believed that private
banks are not concerned about the public demanding its
money back. The private banking management has a scale
of preference of its own, concerning reserves. In some
circumstances of risk or uncertainty, the management of
the private banks may choose to have reserves above the
level legally established, which we will call excess in
reserves. These reserves are not usually turned over
to the central bank. They are under the control of the
private banking system.

Accordingly, then, money supply equal the summation
of currency (C_t) in circulation plus total deposits
$(TD)_t$, that is,

$$(45) \qquad M_{st} = C_t + (TD)_t$$

Also, government issued money is used as currency (C_t),
as a legal reserve (R_t), or as excess in reserve (XR_t),
that is,

$$(46) \qquad H_t = C_t + R_t + XR_t$$

Also, we know that legal reserves (R_t) are a proportion
of the demand deposits, that is,

$$(47) \qquad R_t = \rho TD_t$$

Substituting (47) in (46) and dividing by $(DP)_t$ we have

$$(48) \qquad (\frac{H}{TD})_t = (\frac{C}{TD})_t + \rho + (\frac{XR}{TD})_t$$

where the first term on the right side of equation (48),
the currency of total deposits ratio, $(\frac{C}{DP})_t$, expresses
the public's desires, the second term, the legal reserve
(ρ), expresses the government's scale of preferences,
and the third term, the ratio of excess reserves to
total deposits $(\frac{XR}{TD})_t$ expresses the bank's management
desire with regard to their holding of cash.

The currency to deposit ratio. We will assume the currency to deposit ratio to be a function of the opportunity cost of holding money, which is the interest rate (R_{mex}) and the rate of inflation, that is

$$(49) \quad (\frac{C}{TD})_t = \beta_{11} + \beta_{12} R_{mex} + \beta_{13} \pi_t + U_{7t}$$

where the β's are the parameters to be estimated and U_{7t} is the random error term with the typical assumption. It is expected that the ratio of currency to total deposits $(\frac{C}{TD})$ will move in an opposite direction to the opportunity cost of holding money (R_{mex}), since if the cost of holding cash goes up, it is expected that the public will try to save cash holdings. The inflation rate (Π_t) and the currency to deposit ratio are expected to move in opposite directions.

The ratio of excess of reserves to total deposits. The desired ratio of excess reserves to total deposits $(\frac{XR}{TD}^*)$ are assumed to be negatively related to the opportunity cost of holding money (R_{mex}), and also to be a function of the expected rate of inflation (Π^e_t).

$$(50) \quad (\frac{XR}{TD})^* = \beta_{15} + \beta_{16} R_{mex} + \beta_{17} \pi^e_t$$

The desired excess of reserves to total deposits $(\frac{XR}{TD}^*)$ as presented in (50) is a non-observable variable. In order to have equation (50) expressed only in observable variables, it will be assumed that the changes in adjustment of the ratio of excess reserves to total deposits $(\frac{XR}{TD})$, from one period to another in a proportion of the difference between the level of the desired ratio $(XR^*/TD)_t$, in period t and the actual level of the excess of reserves to total deposits in the previous period $(XR/TD)_{t-1}$, that is,

$$(51) \quad d(\frac{XR}{TD})_t = \delta[(\frac{XR}{TD})^*_t - (\frac{XR}{TD})_{t-1}]$$

where d is a difference operator and the coefficient of adjustment (δ) is expected to lie between zero and one. Developing (51) by the actual ratio of excess reserves to deposit, and substituting the result in equation (50), we have

$$(52) \quad (\frac{XR}{TD})_t = \beta_{17} + \beta_{18} R_{mex} + \beta_{19} (\frac{XR}{TD})_{t-1} +$$
$$+ \beta_{20} \pi^e_t + U_{8t}$$

where

$$\beta_{17} = \delta\beta_{15} \qquad\qquad \beta_{18} = \delta\beta_{16}$$

$$\beta_{19} = (1 - \delta) \qquad\qquad \beta_{20} \quad \delta\beta_{17}$$

Since $\beta_{16} < 0$ and $\beta_{17} < 0$, it is then expected that the parameters will have the following signs:

$$\beta_{18} < 0, \; \beta_{19} \geq 0, \; \beta_{20} < 0$$

Re-arranging equation[21] (45), we have

$$(53) \quad M_{s_t} = [\frac{\frac{C}{TD} + 1}{(\frac{C}{TD})_t + k + (\frac{XR}{TD})_t}] \; H_t$$

where the expression within parenthesis in (53) is the money multiplier. To develop fully the money multiplier equations (49) and (52) can be substituted into (53), which expresses the money supply as a function of the scales of the public's, the government's, and the bank's preferences to hold money.

The monetary base. We mentioned that the monetary base or government issued money (H_t) had two sources: a domestic source and a foreign source. That is,

$$(54) \quad H_t = NFA_t + NDA_t,$$

where NFA_t and NAD_t are the net foreign and net domestic asset holdings of the central bank (El Banco de Mexico).

The Monetary Balance of Payments

Under fixed exchange rates and assuming away sterilization of capital inflows, the monetary balance or overall balance payments, is equivalent to the changes in net foreign assets, and also equal to the summation of its components, that is,

---

[21] For details on the re-arrangement, see the mathematical appendix.

(55) $B_t = d\ NFA_t = (X + OILX)_t - (M + OILM)_t + SCF_t + RIBP_t,$

where B_t is the overall balance of payments, d is a difference operator, NFA_t is net foreign assets held by the central bank -El Banco de Mexico- in period t, X are nominal exports of the non-oil sector, OILX are crude oil exports, M are nominal imports of the non-oil sector, OLIM are imports of the oil sector, SCF are short term capital flows and RIBP are the residual items in balance of payments. (55) could also be expressed in terms of net foreign assets held by the central bank as follows:

(56) $NFA_t = (X + XOIL)_t - (M + OLIM)_t + SCF_t + RIBP_t +$

$+ NFA_{t-1}$

The Inflation Rate

To date, most empirical work on the monetary approach has been conducted under the full employment and small country assumptions,[22] which implies that output and prices are exogenously given and are thus independent of domestic monetary developments. In this section we dispense with the full employment assumption and recognize that at least some prices in the Mexican economy may not immediately respond to world prices. An excess supply of money has thus four "escape valves," namely rising domestic prices after a lag, increasing output, diminishing trade balance and a negative effect on short term capital flows. We have already considered the trade balance effects.

Within the non-oil subsystem is assumed the existence of a sector exposed to international trade, and the existence of a non-traded sector. The exposed sector is assumed to be integrated by industries producing tradable goods. Tradables consists of exportables and importables. Exportables in turn consist of actual exports, as well as of close substitutes for exports that are sold domestically, such as coffee sold to Mexicans. Importables consist of imports as well as

---

[22] See B. Aghlevi and M. Khan, "The Monetary Approach to Balance of Payments Determination, an Empirical Test," in IMF, A Collection of Research Papers, Washington, 1977, p-272

of goods produced domestically and sold domestically
that are close substitutes for imports, such as car
parts produced and sold in Mexico. Domestic prices of
these tradables are determined broadly by the world
market,[24] subject only to tariffs, export subsidies,
international transport costs, and, of course, the ex-
chage rate. The non-traded sector is composed of firms
engaged in the production of non-tradable goods. Non-
tradable goods consist of all those goods and services
the prices of which are determined by supply and demand
domestically. This category consists mainly of services.[25]

Prices of exportable and importable goods will be
aggregated into a single price called "price of tradables" (PT), by assuming a constant price ratio between importables and exportables; while the index price
in the non-tradable sector will be denoted PH.

The domestic price. The aggregate price is a
weighted average of all prices in the economy, however,
for simplicity, we will assume here that the domestic
price (P_t) is the weighted average of the two commodities that exist in the economy: non-tradable and tradable goods, that is,

$$(57) \quad LnP_t = f(PH) \, LnPH + f(PM) \, LnPM$$

where the parameter $f(PH)$ denotes the output share of
non-tradable goods on the GDP deflator,[25] and the
parameter $f(PD)$, the share of tradable goods on the GDP
price deflator. By definition the summation of both
parameters has to be equal to one, that is,

$$(58) \quad f(PH) + f(PM) = 1$$

Expressing (58) in terms of rate of change we have

---

[23]This statement is consistent with the small country assumption,
which we undertook before.

[24]In Mexico for 1978, this sector accounted for about one third
of the GDP. Se J. Lopez Portillo, 2d Informe de Gobierno,
1978.

[25]We are using as price index (Pt) the GDP deflactor of Mexico
and the consumer price index of the United States as PT.

(59) $\frac{1}{P} \frac{dP}{dt} = f(PH) \ (\frac{1}{PH} \frac{dPH}{dt}) + f(PD) \ (\frac{1}{PD} \frac{dPD}{dt})$

where $(1/P \ dP/dt)$ is the observed rate of inflation which has two basic components; the first is the domestic component which is a consequence of weighted changes in prices of non-tradable goods $(\frac{1}{PH} \frac{dPH}{dt})$. The second component is the one produced by weighted changes in the price of importables and exportables consumed domestically $(\frac{1}{PD} \frac{dPD}{dt})$. This component is commonly described as imported inflation, latter defines also as Π_t^i.

Inflation on non-tradable goods is assumed to respond negatively to the gap between potential or normal output $[Y_t^* - (\frac{Y}{P})_t]$ and positively to the rate of expected inflation Π^e, both of which are affected by the prevailing excess of real money stock, that is,

(60) $\frac{1}{PH} \frac{d}{dt}(PH) = \theta_0 + \theta_1 \ [Y_t^* - (\frac{Y}{P})_t] + \theta_2 \ \Pi_t^e$

A larger excess of actual $(\frac{Y}{P})_t$ over potential or normal output (Y_t^*) is expected to increase inflationary pressure on home goods in accordance with the standard Phillips curve argument, and positive inflationaty expectations are assumed also to increase inflationary pressure on home goods, hence the expected signs of the parameters are:

$$0 < \theta_1 \quad , \quad \theta_2 < 1$$

If we now substitute expression (60) into (59) we have

(61) $\frac{1}{P} \frac{dP}{dt} = \beta_{23} + \beta_{24} \ GAP_t + \beta_{25} \ \Pi_t^e + \beta_{26} \ \Pi_t^i + U_{9t}$

where $\frac{1}{P} \frac{dP}{dt}$ is the observed rate of inflation, GAP_t is the gap between normal and current output $[Y_t^* - (\frac{Y}{P})]$ and Π_t^e and Π_t^i are the expected and imported inflation rates. It is also assumed that

$$\beta_{23} = \theta_0 \ f \ (PH)$$
$$\beta_{24} = \theta_1 \ f \ (PM)$$
$$\beta_{25} = \theta_2 \ f \ (PH)$$
$$\beta_{26} = \theta f \ (PD)$$
$$U_{9t} \simeq N \ (0, \ \sigma_u^2)$$

Since $0 < \theta_1, \theta_2 < 0$, $f(PH) > 0$, $f(PM) > 0$, then the expected signs for the parameters to be estimated are:

$$\beta_{24} < 0, \ \beta_{25} > 0, \ \beta_{26} > 0$$

Dynamic Adjustment of the Output

Since monetary factors alone cannot explain the long run real growth of an economy, we incorporate the concept of "normal output" (Y_t^*) which is assumed to be independent of monetary factors and concern ourselves with explaining the short run behavior of the gap between potential (Y_t^*) and actual output $(\frac{Y}{P})_t$.

The $GAP[Y_t^* - (\frac{Y}{P})_t]$ between potential and actual output is assumed to respond negatively to the level of excess demand in the goods market, which is generated by the flow demand for real money $(\frac{D}{P})_t$. In addition, the rate of adjustment of actual output toward its potential level is assumed to depend on the excess of capacity present in the economy, that is:

$$(62) \quad d \ GAP_t = \phi \left(\frac{D}{P}\right)_t + \gamma GAP_{t-1}$$

where $d \ GAP_t$ is the adjustment gap between potential and actual output from one period to another, $(\frac{D}{P})_t$ is the flow demand for real money and GAP_{t-1} is the measure of excess capacity in the previous period. The estimated size of the coeficient ϕ will indicate to what extent an excess real supply of money facing a given real stock demand for cash balances induces an increase in the rate of growth of output in the short run. The estimated value of the parameter γ will be a suggestive empirical test for the presence of the self corrective forces in the process of output determination.

Substituting equation (23) into (62) and developing the expression, we have

$$(63) \ GAP_t = \beta_{28} Y^* + \beta_{29} \left(\frac{M_s}{P}\right) + \beta_{30} GAP_{t-1}$$

where GAP_t is the gap between normal and current output, and $(\frac{M_s}{P})_t$ is real money supply. It is also assumed that

$$\beta_{28} = \frac{\phi(1 - \mu k)}{1 + \phi(1 - \mu k)}$$

$$\beta_{29} = \frac{\phi\mu}{1 + \phi(1 - \mu k)}$$

$$\beta_{30} = \frac{1 + \gamma}{1 + \phi(1 - \mu k)}$$

since $\phi > 0$, $0 < \mu \ k < 1$ and $\gamma > 0$, then the expected sign for the parameters to be estimated are

$$\beta_{28} > 0$$

$$\beta_{29} > 0$$

$$\beta_{30} > 0$$

The Dynamic Adjustment of the International
Capital Flows

We pointed out earlier that an excess of real money supply given a real stock demand for cash balances has several "escape valves." In this section we will develop the fourth "escape valve," namely the capital account. Our approach is a synthesis of the stock equilibrium approach to capital flow derived from Branson[26] and the monetary approach to balance of payments. Capital flows are viewed basically as the mechanism by which a domestic excess supply for money is removed, and consequently key explanatory variables in our model will be those affecting either the demand for or supply of money.

Most recent studies of international capital movements have used the stock-adjustment model developed by Branson[27] who used the Markovitz-Tobin model of portfolio selection to explain the allocation of wealth between domestic and foreign assets.[28] Within this approach the proportion of held foreign assets (FA_t) in a given stock of wealth (W), is a function of the expected yield on foreign assets, compared to alternative yields on domestic assets both measured by foreign and domestic interest rates alternatively, also a function of the risk involved and the size of the stock of wealth, that is,

(64) $FA_t/w = f(R_{mex}, R_{usa}, R_X, W); \quad f_1, f_2, f_4 > 0,$

$$f_3 < 0$$

---

[26] Branson and Hill, p. 34, 1971

[27] Ibid.

[28] See P. Kouri and M. Porter, "International Capital Flows and Portfolio Equilibrium," Journal of Political Economy, 1974, 82, 445.

where R_{mex} and R_{usa} are the domestic and foreign interest rates, respectively RX is the risk involved by holding foreign assets and W is the stock of given wealth.

This basic form, with a variety of additional explanatory variables has been used to explain the net magnitude of net capital flows. This approach has been found to have an econometric problem of simultaneous equation[29] bias which arises where the domestic interest rate is affected by capital flows. A second related problem within this approach is that changes in relative yields between foreign and domestic assets cannot explain capital movements, assuming that both the domestic and foreign are perfect substitutes. Also, that which is relevant for our purposes is not a portfolio shift between domestic and foreign bonds, but between bonds and money.

The basic block to be developed here is an extension of Kouri and Porter's[30] model and an attempt will be made to overcome the criticism raised against the Tobin model, within a more general framework. The block contains equilibrium conditions for the demand and suplly of money, domestic bonds, and foreign bonds.

It will be assumed that in our economy there are three kinds of financial assets:[31] base money, bank money (demand deposits which may not bear interest), domestic bonds and foreign bonds. It is also that expectations regarding the price level are formed according to a learning mechanism, as will be discussed later. The allocation of a given stock of financial wealth between domestic and foreign bonds or money is believed to depend on the domestic stock of wealth, domestic income, the domestic interest rate -the yield on domestic bonds-, the foreign interest -the yield on foreign bonds-, and the degree of speculation. To capture the effects of speculation, dummy variables will be used, based on our previous knowledge of speculation in Mexico.

If domestic and foreign bonds are perfect substitutes, then their respective yields must be equal. However, expectations concerning future changes of the exchange rate will induce transactions to incur a forward cost to cover the risk of devaluation. This means that the foreign and domestic interest rates may differ by

[29] Ibid, p. 446

[30] Ibid.

[31] Kouri and Porter assume only one kind of financial asset: base money.

the amount of the forward cost, that is,

(65) $R_{mex} = R_{usa} + FC$

where FC is the forward premiums. The forward premium in turn is determined by the expected change in the exchange rate (CH) adjusted for risk (RX), that is,

(66) $FC = (CH + RX)$

If we remember, we obtained in expressions (53) and (54) equations for the money supply (M_S) as the following:

$$M_s = mH = m(NDA_t + NFA_t)$$

where M_S is as before, the stock supply of money and Ht the monetary base, m is the money multiplier, and NDA_t and NFA_t are the net domestic and foreign assets held by El Banco de Mexico. The foreign component of the base (NFA_t) may change as a result of a conscious policy of the central bank in order to maintain the exchange rate.

If we recall from (55) the changes in net foreign assets (d NFA_t) are equivalent to the results in the overall balance of payments (Bt), then re-arranging (55) by short term capital flows, we have that

(67) $SCF = d\ NFA_t - CAB_t - RIBP$

where SCF is as before, short term capital movements, d NFA_t are the changes in net foreign assets held by central bank, and CAB_t is current account in balance of payments (X + 0IX) - (M + OILM) and RIBP is other items on the balance of payments. Using (54) in (53) assuming equilibrium in the stock money market in nominal terms, differentiating the equilibrium kY = $m(NDA_t + NFA_t)$ and rearranging the expression in terms of changes in net foreign assets held by the central bank, we have

(68) $d\ NFA_t = \dfrac{k}{m}\ \dfrac{dY}{dt} - \dfrac{d\ NDA_t}{dt}$

where d NFA_t is as before, changes in net foreign assets held by the central bank, k is the proportion of income held in cash balances, m is the money multiplier ($\frac{dY}{dt}$) is the changes in nominal income and $\frac{d}{dt}$ (NDA_t) are the changes in net domestic assets held by the central bank. If we assume the short term capitals to be dependent also on factors such as the changes in the opportunity cost of holding money, hence substituting (68) into (67) and considering the opportunity in equation (67) we have

$$(69) \quad SCF = \frac{\beta 3}{m} + \frac{\beta 4}{m} \, dY_t + \frac{\beta 5}{m} \, dR_{usa} + \frac{\beta 5}{m} \, d \, CH + \frac{\beta 5}{\mu}$$

$$d \, RX + \frac{\beta 6}{m} \, d \, \Pi_t^e - NDA_t + CAB_t$$

Equation (69) simply says that the magnitude of short term capital flow is a function of changes in nominal income (dY_t), changes in the world interest rate, the changes in expected movements in the exchange rate (d CH) and changes in expected risk (d RX). With perfect capital mobility[32] the excess of new supply of securities over domestic acquisition of new securities is absorbed by the world capital market at a fixed rate of interest.

As presented, equation (69) is of analytical use, however, from the empirical viewpoint it calls for a transformation to make the short term capital flow suitable for empirical testing purposes. A reduced form, then, is proposed as follows:

$$(70) \quad SCF = \beta_{32} + \beta_{33} \, d \, (\frac{Y}{P})_t + \beta_{34} \, d \, R_{usa} + \beta_{35} \, d \, CH +$$

$$+ \beta_{36} \, dRX + \beta_{37} \, \Pi_t^e + \beta_{37} \, NDA_t + \beta_{38} +$$

$$+ U_{9t}$$

Since $\beta_4 > 0$, $m > 0$, $\beta_5 < 0$, $\beta_6 > 0$, $\beta_{37} < 0$, β_{39} then the expected coefficients of the parameters to be estimated are:

$$\beta_{33} > 0, \ \beta_{34} < 0, \ \beta_{35} < 0, \ \beta_{36} < 0, \ \beta_{37} < 0,$$

$$\beta_{38} < 0, \ \beta_{39} < 0$$

Long run or normal output. So far we have specified a normal leval or long run level of output without being clear about the meaning of the concept. The rationale behind the specification is as follows:[33] let us assume that the normal or long run output is dependent on a Cobb Douglas type of production function of which cap-

[32]Ibid, P. 25.

[33]For details consult I. Otani, "Inflation in the Open Economy," IMF Staff Papers, 1976, 22, 754.

ital and labor, the factors of production grow at a constant rate over time, that is,

(71) $\quad Y_t^* = A_0 \ K_t^\beta \ L_t^{(1-\beta)}$

where

(72) $\quad K_t = K_0^{\rho g t}$, and

(73) $\quad L_t = L_0^{\rho h t}$

Substituting (72) and (73) into (71) we get

(74) $\quad Y_t^* = A_0 \ K_0^{(\rho g t)\beta} \ L_0^{(\rho h t)(1-\beta)}$

Manipulating (74) and assuming that $Z_0 = K_0 \ L_0$, then we finally have,

(75) $\quad Y_t^* = A_0 \ Z_0^{\rho [\beta g + \ h(1-\beta)]t}$

Since the coefficients were assumed to be constant over time, we are expressing the Y^* only as a function of time, which means that normal or long run output grows constantly over time. Since the nominal interest rate and wage rates are fixed institutionally in Mexico, their actual output can be increased beyond the normal level of output only if an increase in the price level the real interest rate, and the wage rate less than the trend values that are consistent with the nominal level of output.

Estimates for the normal or long run level of output were calculated assuming an adaptation expectation mechanism as follows:

(76) $\quad Y^* - (1 + \ell) \ Y_{t-1}^* = \alpha \ [(\frac{Y}{P})_t - (1 + \ell) \ Y_{t-1}^*]$

where Y^* is the long run or normal level of real output in period t, α is the parameter of adjustment which is assumed to be less than one but greater than zero, ℓ is a parameter that indicates the normal rate of growth of the Mexican economy in real terms.[34]

Equation (76) says that the adjustment of the long run or normal level of output from one period to another depends on the adjustment process between the

---

[34] The "normal" rate of growth of the Mexican economy was set equal to 6.38 percent, and was estimated using a stochastic time series model, developed by the author.

current and the normal levels of output in the previous period, adjusted by the rate of growth (ℓ). Equation (76) can be rearranged such that it can be useful for estimation purposes:

(77) $Y^* = \alpha (\frac{Y}{P})_t + (1 - \alpha)(1 + \ell)\ Y^*_{t-1}$

To estimate the level of normal income in real terms as proposed in equation (77), we had to get rid of the level of normal income lagged on period (Y^*_{t-1}). In order to do so, we lagged the specification in (77) several times. Afterwards, we substituted the lagged values back in (77) in such a way, that Y^* was expressed purely in terms of lagged valves of current income ($\frac{Y}{P}$) plus a lagged of normal income (Y^*) attached to a coefficient whose values were almost zero. ℓ, the rate of growth of normal income in real terms was set equal to 0.638, and values from 0.1 through 0.9 were assumed for α respectively. In this way, ten series were generated for Y^*. All these series were tried in different runs, and finally was selected one which consistently maximized the R^2 as a whole in the econometric model.

The expected rate of inflation. The expected rate of inflation is assumed within this model to be found according to a learning process based on past knowledge of the behavior of the price level. This variable was assumed to be exogenously determined. It was estimated using the following adaptive expectation scheme:

(78) $\Pi^e_t - \Pi^e_{t-1} = \gamma [\Pi_{t-1} - \Pi^e_{t-1}]$

where Π^e_t is the expected rate of inflation in period t, Π_t is the observed rate of inflation, γ is the parameter of adjustment of expectations. Equation (78) implies that the dynamic adjustment of expectation from one period to another is based on what individuals expected to rate of inflation to be and what it really was. For purposes of estimation (6) was mathematically manipulated to yield the following specifications.

(79) $\Pi^e_t = \gamma\ \Pi_{t-1} + (1 - \gamma)\ \Pi^e_{t-1} + W_{2t}$

The actual method used in estimating (79) was to generate nine series each by varying the coefficient of adjustment γ from 0.1 through 0.9 at equal steps of 0.1. These series in turn were used as raw data in the model.

List of Variables

Y_t = Nominal income

C_t = Nominal aggregate consumption

I_t = Nominal aggregate investment

G_t = Nominal aggregate government expenditures

X_t = Value of exports and net services account of the non-oil sector

M_t = Value of imports (excluded oil imports)

P_t = Domestic price level

PX = Price of exports

PM = Price of imports

GA = Aggregate expenditures

d = Difference operator

M*d = Desired amount of stock nominal money balances

D_t = Flow demand for nominal money balances

R_{mex} = Short term interest rates

$\Pi^e{}_t = (\frac{dpe}{P_e})_t$ = Expected rate of inflation

Ms = Nominal stock of money

CR_t = Currency in circulation

TD_t = Total deposit liabilities of commercial banks

CAB = Current account Balance

m = Money multiplier

PH = Price of index of non-tradable goods

RK = Risk factor

H_t = Monetary base

R_t = Required reserves

$(XR)_t$ = Excess reserves of commercial banks

k = Ratio of required reserves to total deposit liabilities of commercial banks

$(\frac{XR}{TD})^{*}_{t}$ = Ratio of desired excess reserves of commercial banks to total deposit liabilities

NFA_t = Net foreign assets holdings of the Banco de Mexico

SCF = Private short-term capital flows

RIB_t = Residual item in the Balance of Payments

RUS = Short term U.S. interest rate

Π_t = Rate of inflation

Y^{*}_{t} = Permanent real income

$n^i = (\frac{dPL}{PL})_t$ = Rate of imported inflation

G^{*}_{t} = Desired government expenditures

GAP = Gap between normal and real current income

IF = Institutional factors

K^{d}_{t} = Level of desired capital stock

3
Empirical Evidence for Mexico

The model was estimated using quarterly data for
Mexico for the period extending from the first quarter
of 1960 to the fourth quarter of 1977. The starting
point of 1960 was chosen for estimation because Mexican
data has been extensively reviewed from that date
onwards by the Bureau of Statistics, now under the
control of the Secretaria de Programacion y Presupuesto,
a government agency in charge of developing an econometric model to fit the needs of the Global Development
Plan 1982-84. Data on income, private consumption,
government expenditures and public and private investment was not available on a quarterly basis, and hence
it was necessary to estimate it. To generate the
quarterly data for the GDP, the index of industrial output was used as an explanatory variables. Consumption
was estimated using the technique provided by TSP[1] to
interpolate time series (INTER) from peak to peak.
Quarterly data on government expenditures was estimated
using the same technique of peak to peak interpolation.
Government investment, was estimated separated from
private investment. In all cases, investment was assumed to be generated by entrepreneurs. The government
was assumed to be an entrepreneur in the activity of
producing development. Aside from that, private
entrepreneurs were regarded as being more sensitive to
the expected rate of inflation than the government, for
investment purposes. Some quarterly data was available
on short term capital flows and balance of payments;

---

[1]Harvard Institute of Economic Research, Time Series Processor
(Version 2.5), Technical Paper No. 12, Cambridge, Mass.,
1974, p. B.12.

the rest had to be estimated using TSP, using the interpolation technique already described.

Because an important purpose of this paper is to
analyze the division of nominal income changes into
prices and output changes, the GNP deflator is used to
deflate all nominal domestic variables, and the Mexican
inflation rate is defined in terms of this index. All
variables related to the world market were deflated in
terms of United States GNP deflators, except oil imports and exports, which were deflated using average
price of Mexican crude oil exports.

The system of equations was kept linear, because
empirical evidence cast in linear form showed itself to
describe adequately the behavior of the Mexican economy,
as can be seen in the result which will be presented
later. Since the system is simultaneous, the two stage
Least Square (2SLS) method of estimation was used to
provide consistent estimates for the parameters of the
system. All equations are corrected for aut-correlation
using the Cochrane-Orcutt iteration method and the t
values are given beneath the coefficients in parenthesis.

AGGREGATE ABSORPTION

Aggregate absorption was originally regarded as a
behavioral equation. However, serious concerns were
raised as to whether such a consolidated variable could
be useful for analytical purposes, since it involved the
complex interactions of different economic agents;
households, government and entrepreneurs who, acting at
the same time and under the same economic conditions,
were expected to have different reactions, which is difficult to deal with in terms of aggregate absorption.
A different standpoint was taken out and it was decided
to break aggregate absorption down into consumption,
government expenditures, private and public or government investment plus imports minus exports. All the
components, except real exports, were treated as
endogenous variables subject to estimation.

It could be worth pointing out that this breakdown
will allow us to analyze more closely the effects of
the different scenarios for each one of the variables,
which will enrich the alternative possibilities for
policy making in Mexico.

Real Private Consumption

This variable deals only with the measured consumption arising out of households. It reflects what will
be called measured consumption which means that it
excludes the household consumption arising out of
government subsidies in Mexico.

$$(1) \quad \left(\frac{C}{P}\right)_t = \underset{(1.64)}{19} + \underset{(12.8)}{0.6} \left(\frac{Y}{P}\right)_t + \underset{(0.55)}{0.53} \left(\frac{MS}{P}\right) -$$

$$- \underset{(3.4)}{123} \; \Pi_t^e$$

$$R^2 = 0.99 \qquad\qquad D.W. = 2.09$$

As the econometric estimation result indicates, real consumption $\left(\frac{C}{P}\right)$ is explained quite well by real income $(Y/P)_t$ and inflation expectations (Π_t^e). Real money supply is a very weak explanatory variable. All the coefficient carry the expected signs and the t's show inflation expectation and real income to be significant at the 0.025 significance level.

The empirical evidence shown in equation (1) seems to lend scant support to the monetarist view which maintains that an unexpected increase in the money supply will encourage people in the short run to adjust their real cash balance holdings by exchanging their excess of money holdings for goods, services and bonds.

The econometric results show that an increase in real income of 1 dollar will produce an increase in private consumption of 60 cents. That is, the marginal propensity to consume out of income is 0.6, which might be regarded as somewhat low.[2] The relevant data for the period under consideration, also shows that real private measured consumption $\left(\frac{C}{P}\right)_t$ has been during the last 20 years a decreasing portion of real domestic absorption $\left(\frac{CA}{P}\right)_t$.[3]

---

[2] Developmental economists tend to believe that the MPC in developing countries is very high, close to one, due to the fact that since income is so low, most of it will be expected to satisfy basic needs.

[3] They exclude consumption of foreign items. For further details on the data consult IMF, Financial Statistics, different issues, or Banco de Mexico, S.A., Estadística de la Oficina de Cuentas de Producción, Mexico, 1977.

It should be noted at the outset that the coefficient for real income does not measure the traditional Keynesian marginal propensity to consume. What we have here is a marginal propensity to consume out of income which embodies the following components:

(2)   MPC = p(1 - kμ)

where p is in an interpretation similar to the straightforward Keynesian multiplier, k, which is the coefficient that measures the properties of income which will be withheld in the form of money, and μ which is the parameter of dynamic adjustment of the flow demand for money. k and μ are expected to depress income and hence to exert a negative influence on the marginal propensity to consume out of real income.

We have already mentioned that we are dealing with "real measured private consumption" (C_p) rather than with realized consumption. Then a possible explanation for the somewhat low marginal propensity to consume out of income in Mexico, is that. Real private consumption as presented here does not account for the large amounts of subsidies granted by the federal government and private institutions, which causes "measured consumption" to under underestimate realized consumption. Another possible explanation for the somewhat low marginal propensity to consume out of real income could be that a high degree of correlation might exist between income and money supply that could make it difficult to disentangle their respective effects on consumption. However, examining the variance-covariance matrix, we found a very low degree of correlation between these two variables.[4] The most plausible explanation for our results seems to be the explanation first outlined.

The expected rate of inflation within our theoretical framework is believed to have two effects on real consumption. First, since the expected price level is expected to change, people adjusting their expectations, e.g. increase their demand for nominal cash holdings lowering consumption. At the same time, changes in the expected price level are expected to induce people to save in cash holdings, e.g. exchange their excess of money holdings by goods and services, increasing real consumption. The final outcome of a change in the expected price level on consumption, then is an empirical

---

[4] The estimate of variance matrices of estimated coefficient are not provided.

matter. In our regression results we found the expected rate of inflation to be very strong explanatory variable for real consumption, with a negative sign.

Within our theoretical framework, an unexpected increase in money supply is believed to create a short run disequilibrium in the stock money market. Households finding themselves with an excess of cash holdings will try to get rid of them by exchanging their excess money holdings for goods and services, increasing in this way their demand for goods and services. Money supply however, turned out to be a very weak explanatory variable.

Real Government Expenditures

$$(3) \quad (\frac{G}{P}) = \underset{(-2.99)}{-6.54} + \underset{(3.45)}{0.014} (\frac{MS}{P})_t + \underset{(4.2)}{0.072} (\frac{Y}{P})_t + \underset{(2.99)}{66} \pi_t^e$$

$$R^2 = 0.97 \qquad\qquad D.W. \ 2.03$$

As the results above indicate, real government expenditures $(\frac{G}{P})$ are explained to a large extent by real income $(Y/P)_t$, and the expected rate of inflation (π_t^e). The money supply $(\frac{MS}{P})_t$ seems to have also strong explanatory power. All the explanatory variables carry the expected signs. It is interesting to note that the expected rate of inflation was found to be statistically significant at the 0.025 confidence level, and to carry a positive sign, in spite of some theoretical considerations which suggest that government as such does not form future expectations concerning the price level.[5]

The marginal propensity to consume government expenditures $(\frac{G}{P})_t$ out of real income $(\frac{Y}{P})_t$ is a complex parameter wichi includes the following effects:

$$(4) \quad MPG = gn(1 - \mu k)$$

[5] J. Atta, "A Macroeconomic Model of Ghana: Simulation experiments in Large Scale Econometric Building for a Developing Country," doctoral dissertation, University of Colorado. 1979. Ann Arbor, Michigan: Univ. Microfilm, 1980.

where g represents the dynamic adjustment of government
expenditures from one period to another, n is the marginal propensity to consume government expenditures out
of real income, $(\frac{Y}{P})_t$ and μ is the coefficient which
measures the adjustment in government desires to hold
cash balances due to unexpected changes in the money
supply.[6] k measures the proportion of income held in
the form of cash balances. k and μ tend to depress the
marginal propensity to consume government expenditures
out of changes in money supply.

The empirical results seem to suggest that government expenditures are quite well explained within our
theoretical framework which at first included as an additional explanatory variable the net result in current
accounts in balance of payments, a variable which was
expected to capture government subsidies, which in light
of the current population increase and the decline in
the rate of growth of agricultural production, have been
channeled to the world market. However, further careful
thought[7] reveled that causality was running from government expenditures to balance of payments, rather than
the reverse which was the first specification.

Real Private Investment

Real private investment $(\frac{PI}{P})_t$ was cast in gross terms.
Real private investment was considered to be a function
of the desired level of capital stock by entrepreneurs.
Since the desired level of capital is unobserved, we further assumed that the adjustment in the desired level of
capital was a function of the performance of the economy

---

[6]This statement is valid, since according to the theoretical
framework developed here, the government does not have control
of the money supply and hence it is possible for government
officials to face unexpected changes in money supply. The
government is assumed to have only the control of the domestic
component of the monetary base. The money supply is regarded
as being jointly determined by the desires of the public, the
government, and the bankers.

[7]The author owes this correction to J.K. Atta, who pointed out
to me the incorrections in the former specification.

in the past, measured by the level of aggregate absorption adjusted by the expectations held by entrepreneurs. Altogether, these led us to the following specifications for real private investment from which the following results were obtained:

$$(5) \quad (\frac{PI}{P}) = \frac{-12.06}{(-0.72)} + \frac{0.32}{(1.42)} (\frac{Y}{P})_{t-1} - \frac{0.19}{(-2.55)} (\frac{Y}{P})_{t-2} -$$

$$- \frac{0.336}{(-0.65)} (\frac{MS}{P})_{t-1} + \frac{0.64}{(0.89)} (\frac{MS}{P})_{t-2} -$$

$$- \frac{0.045}{(0.89)} \pi_t^e$$

$$R^2 = 0.90 \qquad\qquad D.W.\ 1.70$$

The specifications designed for real private investment $(\frac{PI}{P})_t$ seems to explain it well. However, the parameters for real money supply lagged do not carry the expected signs. The expected rate of inflation has a weak explanatory power.

The coefficients for real income lagged one period, $(Y/P)_{t-1}$, embodies the following effects:

$$(6) \quad i_1 = \alpha (1 - \mu k)$$

where α is the parameter which measures the dynamic adjustment in the desired stock of capital in response to the past level of economic activity measured by the level of real absorption. μ and k are as explained before, and again both are expected to depress investment. The empirical finding is consistent with our theoretical framework.

The parameters for real income lagged two quarters $(Y/P)_{t-2}$, is also a complex arrangement which includes the following effects:

$$(7) \quad i_2 = \alpha h (1 - \mu k)$$

where α, μ and k are as before, and h is the parameter of adjustment which measures the impact of present and past levels of desired stock of capital in current investment. h is assumed to decline geometrically as the size of the lag increase.

The parameter for money supply lagged one period includes the following effects:

$$(8) \quad i_3 = \alpha\mu$$

where α and μ are as explained before.

Within our framework it is believed that an unexpected increase in the money supply will result in a dis
equilibrium in the stock money market,[8] which will gener
ate a negative flow demand for money, which is expected
to increase demand for goods and bonds. The increase in
the demand for goods is expected to raise the level of
aggregate abosrption, which in turn will raise the level
of desired capital stock, and hence the level of private
investment. The excess of demand in the good market on
the other hand, is expected to generate with a lag some
increase in the price level as a consequence of closing
the gap between permanent or normal income and current
real income. The increase in the price level is of
itself expected to generate some adjustment in the
stock money market by raising the amount of nominal money required to adjust the real cash balances to the
price level, generating in this way a reverse in the
flow demand for money, which will return the money market to equilibrium.

The flow demand for money channeled to the domestic
bond market will result in an excess demand for domestic
bonds, which will increase the price of bonds and will
lower the interest rate, which is regarded as an opportunity cost of holding money. The lowering in the interest rate in turn is expected to raise the demand for
money. The domestic bond market in this way will provide
another force which will help to restore equilibrium in
the money market.

The excess demand for bonds will in turn affect the
foreign market. The demand for foreign bonds will imply an outflow of money, which is expected to affect
negatively the monetary balance of payments, which in
turn will lower the monetary base and hence the money
supply.

In this way we have several forces working to return
the stock money market to the equilibrium position.

Government Investment

In the first chapter of this work we mentioned that
the rate of population growth for Mexico has been above
3 percent per annum. Under these circumstances, a demanding need in the country is not only to maintain the
current population employed as is typically the case in

---

[8] Assuming that before the unexpected increase in the money supply,
the stock money market was in equilibrium.

most developed countries where the main concern is to
maintain the people who are actually employed in their
employment. Creation of new jobs is not so much a problem in light of the small rate of growth in the labor
force. However, in Mexico problems with the labor market are twofold: one is to maintain the pople who are
already employed in their jobs, and the second to create
enough new jobs to keep pace with the dynamics of the
labor force. To solve the first problem, powerful laws
(la Ley Federal del Trabajo) with the stature of consti-
tutional law have been issued to encourage employers to
maintain their employees' employment.

The creation of new jobs has been linked, among
other things, to the level of investment. Investment
has to be carried out, not only because it increase the
social wealth and helps to provide a larger amount of
goods and services, but also because net investment
provides new employment opportunities.

In the period under consideration, investment has
been carried out in a large proportion by private investors. The role of the government has been also very
important, even though of a lesser magnitude, hence
creation of new employment opportunities was mostly provided by the private sector. After 1973, and more
critically in 1976 and 1977, private investment fell
and government investment rose. This circumstances
suggests that government, acting as an entrepreneur pro-
moting economic development, will become more significant as an investor when the level of "capital stock"
is not expected to reach the desired level, where the
desired level of capital stock again is to be measured
by the past performance of the economy. But contrary
to the reaction function of the private investor, the
government is expected to invest more the poorer the
economic performance measured in terms of aggregate
absorption, since it feels compelled to fill the
vacuum in investment needs and hence employment opportunities, left by private investors reluctant to invest, when they are facing an excess of "desired capital
stock."

According to the empirical results, for real investment we obtain the following results:

$$(9) \quad (\tfrac{GI}{P})_t = \begin{array}{c} -26.5 \\ (-4.61) \end{array} + \begin{array}{c} 0.348 \\ (2.93) \end{array} (\tfrac{Y}{P})_{t-1} - \begin{array}{c} 0.136 \\ (-1.26) \end{array} (\tfrac{Y}{P})_{t-2}$$

$$+ \begin{array}{c} 0.018 \\ (0.03) \end{array} (\tfrac{MS}{P})_{t-1} + \begin{array}{c} 1.76 \\ (-2.97) \end{array} (\tfrac{MS}{P})_{t-2}$$

$$R^2 = 0.86 \qquad\qquad D.W. - 2.58$$

As can be seen, the specifications designed to explain government investment suggested by abstract reason
ing and economic theory, explained well the endogenous
variable. What is even more interesting is to note that
in the key variable we get signs opposite in direction
to those obtained for private investment. For instance,
private investors apparently reacted, as expected, positively to high levels of past income, whereas government
investment reacted negatively to good past performances
of the economy, as we hypothesized. The result for real
public investment also seems to be consistent with the
institutional conditions of the country where an important portion of government expenditures and government
investment are financed through domestic money creation
lagged.

Real Imports

$$(10) \quad (\frac{M}{PM})_t = \frac{23.031}{(2.2)} - \frac{29.449.7}{(2.5)} (\frac{PM}{P})_t + \frac{0.93E-04}{(6.45)} (\frac{GA}{P})_t$$

$$R^2 = 0.92 \qquad D.W. = 1.69$$

Real imports seem to be explained quite well by the
relative prices (PM/P) between Mexico and the United
States[9] and by real aggregate absorption which was used
as an explanatory variable and which will allow us to
relate imports to both of goods (foreign and domestic).
Economic theory suggests that if the domestic price
(P_t) grows faster than the world price, represented by
the United States price level (PM), then Mexican con-
sumers will find that domestic goods are relatively more
expensive than their foreign substitutes, and then will
turn to substituting the cheaper foreign counterpart for
the domestic good. For Mexico, it seems to be the case
that the percent change in the domestic price, relative
to the United States price index, has a heavy impact on
imports, whereas an increase of one peso in real aggregate expenditures is expected to generate a small increase in imports net of oil. Empirical evidence points
out the importance of relative prices to determine

[9] Seventy-three percent of Mexico's imports and exports
are traded with the United States.

Mexican imports net of oil.

According to our conceptual framework, an unexpected increase in the money supply is expected to generate a negative flow demand for money or an excess demand in the goods and bonds markets which in turn generates an increase in the domestic price level by affecting the prices of non-tradable goods, non-importable and non-exportable goods. Since the world price represented by the United States price is assumed to be parametric, the increase in the domestic price level will negatively affect the relative prices, generating in this way a relative rise in the demand for foreign goods. The increased amount of imports in turn will negatively affect the current account balance, the monetary base, and finally the money supply, providing some forces which will pull the stock money market back to equilibrium.

The negative flow demand for money reflected is expected to induce an excess demand in the goods market, which will raise the level of aggregate expenditures, a portion of which will be expenditures on foreign goods. The increased expenditures on foreign goods will represent an increased amount of imports which in turn may induce a deficit in current account, a deficit in the overall balance of pauments, a decrease in net foreign assets held by the central bank (El Banco de Mexico), a decrease in the monetary base, and finally the stock money supply. This process provides another force which will tend to resotre the equilibrium in the stock money market.

In general terms, it can be said that to break down aggregate absorption into its components added much to this work, since it allowed analysis of the reaction of the different economic agents acting within the Mexican economic environment. A good example of the empirical and theoretical gains of the breakdown are the results for investment, which showed, as expected, the government as investor acting in a different manner than a private investor would be expected to do.

In general terms, we can say that the components of aggregate absorption, and hence aggregate absorption, are well explained by the econometric specifications designed for that purpose, which will be used as a base for simulation experimentation in the latter part of this chapter.

Income and Excess Capacity

Real income and real aggregate absorption are expected to be identical in the absence of disequilibrium in the stock money market, where income has been defined according to the standard national accounting specification. Within this block, the GAP concept is developed. The composite variable GAP[10] is assumed to be equal to real normal income[11] minus real current income

(11) $(\frac{GAP}{P})_t = \underset{(1.39)}{2898} - \underset{(-2.12)}{0.278} (\frac{MS}{P})_{t-1} +$

$+ \underset{(2.85}{0.055} Y* + \underset{(3.03)}{0.71} (\frac{GAP}{P})_{t-1}$

$R^2 = 0.84$ \hspace{2cm} D.W. = 2.06

The gap is well explained by the real money supply lagged one quarter, $(MS/P)_{t-1}$, the normal or permanent income $(Y*)$, and the gap lagged one quarter. In equation (11) the coefficient for normal or permanent income is not a critical one, since normal income was the result of a variable transformation devised and carried out to avoid having current real income $(\frac{Y}{P})_t$ as an explanatory variable, which is the endogenous variable on the right hand side of the equation (11). Much more importance is attached to the remaining coefficients.

An unexpected increase in the money supply is expected to create a disequilibrium in the stock money market. People trying to get rid of these excess cash balances will generate a negative flow demand for money, which is expected to be partially reflected in a higher demand for domestic goods, and an increase with a lag in the price level which is expected to encourage in the

---

[10] The gap concept is similar to that developed by M. Khan, "A Monetary Model of Balance of Payment," *Journal of Monetary Economics*, 1975, 2, 316. See also B. Aghlevi and C. Rodriguez, "Trade Prices and Output in Japan: A Simple Monetary Model," *IMF Staff Papers*, March 1980, p. 43.

[11] Real Normal Income is a concept in line with Friedman's permanent income. See M. Friedman, *A Theory of Consumption*, National Bureau of Economic Research, Princeton University Press, 1957. Also similar to Laidler's concept employment, see D.W. Laidler, "The Permanent Income Concept in a Macroeconomic Model", *Oxford Economic Papers*, March 1968.

in the short run entrepreneurs to increase their supply of domestic goods, before they adjust their expectations and hence to close the gap between normal or permanent income and current income.[12] This implies that we expect the gap to move in an opposite direction to the money supply, which is the result shown in the empirical evidence. The increase in the price level and the increase in imports will raise the stock demand for money and worsen the current account of balance. Both effects will feed back into the stock money supply and demand until equilibrium is reached in the stock money market, and the flow demand for money becomes zero. All these effects are simulated in the latter part of this chapter.

Prices and Inflation

The rate of inflation in Mexico is assumed to depend on domestic and foreign factors. Domestic or internal factors are, first, the expected rate of inflation, which is assumed to depend on past levels of inflation adjusted by expectation, and second, the gap between normal or permanent income and current income which has been discussed. External or foreign factors affecting the rate of inflation are the rate of change in the price index of imports and exports, which is assumed to be measured by the United States GDP price deflator. For inflation the following results were obtained:

$$(12) \quad \Pi = \begin{array}{c} 0.049 \\ (1.90) \end{array} + \begin{array}{c} 1.28 \\ (6.34) \end{array} \Pi^e + \begin{array}{c} 0.20 \\ (1.89) \end{array} \Pi^i - \begin{array}{c} 0.83 \\ (-2.13) \end{array} GAP_t$$

$$\begin{array}{c} -05E \\ GAP_{t-1} \end{array}$$

$$R^2 = 0.97 \qquad\qquad D.W. = 2.00$$

From the results we can see that the inflation rate in Mexico is well explained by the expected rate of inflation and imported inflation, which carry the correct signs. The composite variable gap has the correct sign and is significant at the 0.025 confidence level.

---

[12] This is true only if before the increase in the money supply there were some unused resources and the increase in the money supply is truly unexpected. The increase in the supply of money will be partially reflected in an overshooting of the economy, by having current real income surpassing normal or permanent income.

The results out of equation (12) suggest that instrumental variables to fight inflation are the "imported"
and expected rates of inflation. The first variable Π^i
is out of control, since Mexican authorities can do nothing to prevent the world price from rising, since the
world price is parametric and determined by the world
market in which Mexico is a small competitor.

With regard to the expected rate of inflation, this
is also a very difficult variable to deal with, given
the many psychological consideration which enter into
its determination, such as how to convence people in a
current inflationary environment that the future rate of
inflation for some unconvincing reason will be lower than
the current rate. A good example of the difficultness to
extract inflationary expectations from people's minds is
vividly reflected in the current attitude of the middle
aged, middle class Mexican who grew up and lived up most
of his life with growth and stability and who now regards
inflation as a "natural" phenomenon.

For the reasons expressed above, we are led to believe that if the results shown by empirical evidence are
as true as they seem to be, then inflation will remain
with us for the time being, with little hope of defeating
it.

The Monetary Sector

In this block we are mainly interested in isolating
the more important factors which determine the money
supply, among the complexities arising out of the Mexican
monetary sector. First of all, in the process of ab-
stracting, we were led to conclude that the money supply
is the product of the monetary base and the money multiplier. The monetary base was assumed to have a foreign
and domestic component, the first of these being available to the government to somewhat influence the money
supply, and the second assumed to be identical to the
changes in net foreign assets held by the central bank.
The monetary multiplier has been assumed to be generated
by the joint influence of the public, the banking management, and government officials through the legal reserve,
which is another tool of monetary policy available to
them.

The currency to deposit ratio. The currency to deposit ratio is assumed to reflect people's influence
in money supply creation, and its econometric specification is reflected in equation (13) below:

$$(13) \quad (\frac{C}{TD})_t = \begin{array}{c} 0.5 \\ (24) \end{array} - \begin{array}{c} 1.27 \\ (-4) \end{array} \Pi - \begin{array}{c} 0.0012 \\ (-0.3) \end{array} RUS -$$

$$\frac{0.012}{(-2.78)} \text{ DUMMY } 1 - \frac{0.019}{(-4.09)} \text{ DUMMY } 2 -$$

$$\frac{-0.026}{(7.09)} \text{ DUMMY } 3 + \frac{0.08}{(3.72)} \text{ DUMMY } 38 +$$

$$\frac{0.12}{(5.43)} \text{ DUMMY } 72$$

$$R^2 = 0.82 \qquad\qquad D.W. = 2.19$$

It is particularly interesting to note that the values of the R^2 coefficient are high, even though the endogenous variable exhibits a large degree of fluctuation with no apparent trend in its movements. All the estimated coefficients have the correct sign and most are significant at the 0.025 confidence level. It is also interesting to note that the explanatory power exhibited in the current rate of inflation, where a one point increase in the inflation rate is expected to decrease the ratio by 1.2 points, which is a reasonable result, considering inflation is a cost of holding money.

The interest rate is another cost of holding money, measured by the foreign income. Since the short term interest seems not to have been allowed to reflect money market considerations in Mexico, we assumed that the domestic short-term interest plus some factor to account for risk differential, expected changes in the exchange rate and institutional consideration would be equal to the United States short term interest rate on treasury bonds, that is,

(14) $R_{mex} = RUS + IF$

where IF was measured by the set of dummy variables.

From the results, we can see that institutional considerations as part of the Mexican short term interest rate play an important role in determining the currency to deposit ratio. For instance DUMMY 38 was deemed to reflect all the fears and disturbances that arose from the student revolt in 1968, and more than that, the change in the leadership of the country. The beginning of the political campaign of the candidate Luis Echeverria[13] was surrounded by controvery in many areas and

---

[13] Luis Echeverria was elected Mexican President to be in office from January, 1970 through December, 1976.

ended in economic turmoil in 1976. The last period was
expected to be captured by other dummy variable (DUMMY
72). The remaining set of dummy variables (D1, D2, D3)
were used to deseasonalize the data.

As a general assessment, we can say that the currency
to deposit ratio is highly influenced by the level of the
rate of inflation and the "Mexican interest rate" according to the way in which we have defined it.

The Excess Reserve to Total Deposits. This was a very
difficult behavioral equation to deal with, given the
difficulties in measuring it, and the highly complex set
of influences which seem to determine it.

$$(\frac{XR}{TD})_t = \underset{(1.35)}{0.02} + \underset{(0.42)}{0.00075} \Pi^e - \underset{(-0.29)}{0.005} RUS +$$

$$\underset{(0.58)}{0.01} DUMMY\ 65 + \underset{(0.68)}{0.034} DUMMY\ 68 +$$

$$\underset{(4.41)}{0.018} DUMMY\ 1 - \underset{(-3.76)}{0.015} DUMMY\ 2 -$$

$$\underset{(-2.42)}{0.015} DUMMY\ 3 + \underset{(1.4)}{0.89} (XR/TD)_{t-1}$$

$$R^2 = 0.89 \qquad\qquad D.W. = 2.07$$

It is highly interesting to note that the value of
the R^2 is quite high in spite of the vagaries of the behavior of the endogenous variable, which seems to be
inconclusive. It is also highly surprising that the behavior of the ratio in excess of reserves to total
deposit is mostly explained by seasonal considerations.
This kind of finding may have two possible explanations,
which are not mutually exclusive. The first explanation
might be that the results are simply reflecting the procedure by which the raw data was estimated[14], or else
that the data reflects the higher demand for cash by the
public during the different season, which leads the

---

[14]Raw data on time and demand deposit was obtained quarterly from
the IMF statistics and the Banco de Mexico annual report. We
only assumed the value of the legal reserve, which does not
seem to have been an important variable in the outcome.

banking officials to hold a reserve in excess of what is
required in order to satisfy the demand for cash during
the season. We believe the second explanation seems to
have enough common sense to be credible. Then the set
of seasonal dummy variables are in fact reflecting economic considerations with regard to the level of economic
activity in the country.

The Money Supply, Some Considerations. Once we have
developed estimates for the currency to total deposit
ratio and the excess in reserve to total deposit ratio,
we are ready to make some estimates on the monetary
multiplier which will be used for purposes of the simu-
lations later. To have derived totally the money supply,
what was needed was information on the net foreign and
domestic assets held by the central bank. This type of
specification will allow us to link the monetary base and
hence the money supply creation to the balance of payments. The overall result in balance of payments or the
result in the monetary balance was regarded as identical
to the changes in net foreign assets held by El Banco de
Mexico or alternatively, the net foreign assets in the
current period to be identical to the overall result in
the monetary balance plus the net foreign assets held by
the central bank lagged one period. In this way, we have
the balance of payments affecting the money supply, and
this in turn affecting the monetary market and producing
disturbances which are expected to generate a flow demand
for money which is to be partially reflected in changes
in the price level, the size of the gap, the current
account balance and the flows of capital, until equi-
iibrium is reached again, in a fashion already described.

The Balance of Payments

In this block of the system, we attempt to develop
some understanding of the process of determination of
balance of payments and the way it affects, and is affected by other variables of the system.
The current account is regarded simply as the difference between total exports minus total imports. From
these components, we have already reached the result for
the imports equation, which was embodied as a component
of aggregate absorption earlier in this chapter.
From the capital account we turn our attention to
the variables affecting the short term capital movements,
which include error and omission as a component. The
long term capital movements and other items of balance
of payments were included in one single residual variable denominated other items in the balance of payments.

Short term capital flows. Short term capital flows
have been shown in the past to be important element of
monetary instability in Mexico, and here we give attention to them in an attempt to discover a set of explanatory variables capable of explaining the behavior of
short term capital flows. Following a process of ab-
straction shown in Appendix A, which is more thoroughly
explained in Chapter 2, we arrived at the following
specifications where the results are as follows:

$$(16) \quad SCF = \frac{57.29}{(2.96)} - \frac{0.0017}{(1.76)} \, dY_t - \frac{0.0043}{(-4.32)} TB - $$

$$\frac{44}{(-2.84)} \, d \, RUS$$

$$R^2 = 0.80 \qquad\qquad D.W. = 2.8$$

The results seem to explain well the behavior of
short term capital flows in spite of the tremandous fluctuations that the endogenous variable has experienced.
An interesting finding arising out of the empirical
evidence is that a change in nominal income (dY_t) generates an outflow of capital. The reason behind the
finding is that an unexpected change in nominal income
will induce people to believe that they have a larger
command over goods and services. In the short run,
among other things, this will lead them to demand more
cash balances to maintain a constant proportion of the
income in the form of cash balances, since the income
elasticity in the demand for cash balances is assumed
to be equal to one. Second, they will be induced to
adjust their demand for goods and services and for
foreign and domestic bonds, where bonds are assumed to
be a superior good. This implies that the unexpected
increase in nominal income will induce an excess demand
in the foreing and domestic bond market, where the
excess demand in the foreign bond market is expected
to have a counterpart in an outflow of short term capital
flows, an explanation which seems to be consistent with
the findings.
A second interesting finding is the reported negative relationship between the world short run interest
rate (R_{usa}) and the short term capital flows. If we
recall we assumed the United States interest rate to be
a measure of world interest rates, to which the short
term Mexican interest rate should be related. The dif-
ferences between them are the result of market imper-
fections and risk differential. Hence if the world
interest is an approximate measure of the opportunity
cost of holding money in Mexico, then a change in the

opportunity cost of holding money represented by a raise in the short term interest rate is expected to induce people to adjust their cash holdings, generating in this way an excess demand for goods and for domestic and foreign bonds. The excess demand in the foreign bond market will have as a counterpart in the short run an outflow of capital an explanation which is again consistent with our findings.

Some final comments on the balance of payments. The econometric specifications set up to explain some of the components of the balance of payments seem to work well enough to describe the behavior of the endogenous variables under consideration, in spite of the fluctuations and sudden changes in direction that they seem to take.

THE SIMULATION OF THE MODEL

The last part of this chapter will be devoted to the analysis of the econometric model converted to a simulation model, which is linear[15] in parameters and non-linear in variables.

The model contains blocks explaining the dynamic behavior of aggregate absorption in real terms, the level of national income in nominal and real terms, the level of excess of productive capacity for the mexican economy represented by the difference between normal or expected national income and current real income, the general price level, inflation, money supply, current account balance of payments and short term capital flows. The key policy variables of the model are the price (expressed in Mexican pesos) and the volume of crude oil exports of PEMEX, the national oil company. Both variables are expected to affect the level of money supply via the current account of balance of payments and from then on the level of economic activity. Other important policy variable affecting the level of money supply within this model is the level of legal reserves required on demand and time deposits, which for simplicity was assumed to be fixed within the si-

---

[15]The linearity in parameter of the simulation model is in line with the structural econometric model which is linear in variables and linear in parameters.

mulation period.

The model as presented, was run under three different set of scenarios designed to explore and test the dynamic impact of oil revenues in the non-oil sector of the Mexican economy.

THE SIMULATION SCENARIOS

Several sets of scenarios were tried, to allow us to come up with some basic conclusions about the near future of the Mexican economy given certain conditions.

The first set contains three scenarios and it is labeled, "The Lack of Government Spending". In all the cases for this set it was assumed, for the period under consideration, a mild level of inflationary expectations, a fixed level of legal reserves for demand and time deposits, a conservative rate of growth for the domestic component of the monetary base and finally, government spending to be unrelated to the level of real income and economic growth. This first scenario was designed to test the importance of oil revenues to lift by itself under different conditions the Mexican economy, in the absence of a dynamic government expenditures and government investment.

The second set of scenarios fully incorporates public expenditures and let them grow according to their historical pattern. Also for all the two different scenarios it is assumed the same rate of growth for the domestic component of the monetary base. The rate of growth of this last variable is assumed to be below what it has been its historical pattern. Finally, for the first scenario it is additionally assumed a mild level of inflationary expectations, in contrast with the second scenario, where a high level of inflationary expectations are undertaken.

The third set of scenarios fully incorporates public expenditures, and mild and high levels of inflationary expectations as we did in the previous scenario set. But for this set, it is additionally assumed for all the scenarios an aggresive rate of growth for the domestic component of the monetary base.

"The Lack of Government Spending": Scenario Set.

This set contains scenario 4 which was labeled "The Dynamic of the Stationary State"; scenario 5 which was named "The varying Oil Revenues Over Time"; and scenario 6 which is identified as "The Historical Trend"

"The Dynamic of the Stationary State": Scenario (4)

This scenario is labeled in this way, because we assume a once and for all change in crude oil exports, inflationary expectations, normal income, and the world interest rate. The change in all these variables was based on their growth rate. The results out of this run

104

for terms of trade between Mexico and the United States,
Nominal income, Real national income, Real aggregate
absorption, Real private consumption, Real government
consumption, Real government investment, Real private in
vestment, Real imports, the rate of inflation, are presented in graphic #1 through graphic #10 in Appendix A
by curves showing as sub index the number
four[16].

The analysis of the results from this scenario shows
that the level of real income and the level of aggregate
absorption remain stagnant for a period of two years.
Afterwards the levels of this variables are raised moder
ately just to fall down after the forth period. The
trend of these variables over time suggests that the
price block responds quickly to the changes in inflation
ary expectation, whereas the real block (aggregate expenditures or real national income and its components)
responded somewhat slowly and weakly to the changes on
all policy variables. According with graphics 2 and 3,
real income and real aggregate absorption responded to
the incentives very weakly only after three years, just
to slow down afterwards.

As an assesment of the results for this scenario,
we can say that the lack of government spending causes
the economy to stagnate; also that monetary and price
variable react quickly to the changes operated on the
exogenous variables, whereas the real variable take from
two to three years to pick up temporarily and then fade
afterwards.

The Varying Oil Revenues Over Time": Scenario (5)

Within this scenario crude oil exports, growing at
a steady rate of 20% per year, is the only instrumental
policy variable allowed to change. The rest of the exogenous variables remain constant.

The results out of this scenario represented in
graphics #1 through 10 by the curves subindexed with

---

[16]Let us suppose we want to know the behavior of real national
income (YNC) within the period under consideration, first of
all, we find out graphic #2, labeled "Real National Income
(YNC) and then on it we locate curve Y_4. The same procedure
can be applied to find out about the dynamic behavior of any
other endogenous variable of our model.

number five, seem to suggest that the response of monetary and price variables to the oil revenues incentives
are very quick, whereas the real variable (real national
income and its components) take from three to four years
to respond to the persistence of growing in oil revenues.
Interesting to note, is that as the time runs, real aggregate absorption and real national income tend to converge, to remain close to equilibrium afterwards. This
finding seems to lend support to the monetary view, that
if the economy is allowed to operate, it will self correct making use of a built in stability mechanism. This
pattern toward equilibrium it is more clearly seen when
the rate of inflation has stabilized and the economic
agents are able to realize their expectations and foresee
the future outcome with a higher degree of confidence.
However, this self corrective mechanis seems to take
from four to five years to operate, which from the insti
tutional perspective in Mexico is a very long period of
time to wait for.
     As a general assessment of this scenario we can say
that persistent oil revenues given a constant level of
inflation and a very conservative management of the mone
tary policy, are able to raise the level of economic
activity in spite of a lack of government spending. The
dynamic response of real variables is again slow and
requires from three to four years to pick up from then
on.

"The Historical Trend": Scenario (6)

     Within this scenario crude oil exports are allowed
to change at a steady rate of 20 percent yearly. The
expected rate of inflation, normal income, the U.S.
interest rate and the amount of net assets held by the
central bank (the domestic component of the monetary
base) are assumed to grow according to their rates of
growth. The level of legal reserves on demand and time
deposits is assumed to remain constant. The results of
this scenario are represented in graphics #1 through 10
by the curves subindexed with the number six.
     According to the runs of this scenario we can see
that during the two first periods the level of economic
activity slightly declines as it happened with the two
previous scenarios. By the third year economic activity
recovers slightly but declines steadily afterwards.
     As an assessment of the results of this scenario, we
can say that a Mexican economy fed with persistent oil
revenues and mild inflationary expectations facing a
lack of government spending most likely will remain
stagnant with little hopes of change.
     As a general assessment of the results from this set
of scenarios, we can conclude that with relative price

stability and oil exports growing at a rate of 20% per
year the Mexican economy grows even in the absence of
government spending. The runs also suggest that economic growth arising out of oil revenues can be retarded or
even prevented as a result of price instability coming
out of inflationary expectation and the growth of the
domestic component of the monetary base. Inflation appears to exert a very pervasive influence by providing a
very uncertain environment for economic agents. We can
also conclude that there seem to be some evidence to
support the conclusion that the Mexican economy pos-
sesses a self corrective stability mechanism, which requires three to four years to work out, given price
stability.

"The Unconstrained Model":Scenarios Set

     This set contains scenario 1, which was labeled
"Varying Oil Revenues", scenario 2 which was named
"Varying Oil Revenues under Mild Inflationary Expectations", and scenario 3 which is identified as "Varying
Oil Revenues under Inflationary Expectations."
     The assumptions ruling this set are very similar to
those held in the previous set of scenarios, except that in
this section we are fully integrating government spending in the simulation runs.

"Varying Oil Revenues":Scenario (1)

     This scenario was designed to test the importance
of crude oil exports to lift the Mexican economy given
a dynamic role of government investment and public
expenditures.
     Crude oil exports growing at a steady rate of 20
percent yearly is the only variable allowed to change.
The remaining exogenous variable are assumed constant.
     According with the results out of the simulation
presented in graphic #1 thorough 10 by curves subindexed
by the number one. We can see that during the first
three years the response of aggregate absorption to the
steady increase of 20% per year of crude oil export is
very slow. By the forth year real aggregate absorption
takes off very strongly just to keep the same pace of
growth afterwards. The same behavior is observed on
real national income. Important to note is that all
the components of this last variable (real private
consumption, real government consumption real and private investment) grow also in a steady fashion. The
current rate of inflation[1] also maintains a very stable

---

[1]The current rate of inflation is an endogenous variable, which
should not be confused with the expected rate of inflation which
is an exogenous variable.

pattern of growth.

The results coming out of this simulation run, suggest that crude oil exports growing at a steady rate of 20 percent yearly raises the level of economic activity, as we had had before in the second run of the previous set of scenarios. However, now the participation of government spending given price stability, greatly improves the performance of the Mexican economy. A simple inspection of the graphical results at the end of this chapter, will show us also, that the best performance of the Mexican economy is obtained under the assumption of this scenario.

"Varying Oil Revenues Under Mild Inflationary Expectations": Scenario (2)

Within this scenario as the title indicates, two policy variables are instrumented: Oil revenues and inflationary expectations. The results for the scenario are shown on the curves subindexed with the number two. Real incomes as before takes two years to respond to the inflow of oil revenues, just to grow moderately afterwards and finally to take off after the fifth period. The same behavior is reported for real aggregate absorption and the components of both of the previous variables. The current rate of inflation shows a smooth cyclical behavior during the first five periods just to settle afterwards.

As an overall assessment of this scenario, we can say that the allowance for mild inflationary expectation affects the overall performance of the Mexican economy. Mild inflationary expectations yield to a generl level of economic activity inferior to that obtained in the previous run.

"Varying Oil Revenues Under Inflationary Expectations": Scenario (3)

The policy variables operated are again oil revenues and inflationary expectations. The results arising of the simulation run described on the graphics #1 to 10 by the curves subindexed with the number three, seem to indicate, clearly, that a higher level of inflationary expectation produces a more ciclical behavior of the Mexican economy and levels of economic activity more modest than those reported in the two previous scenarios.

The economy, as before, takes two years to respond to the steady increase of oil revenues inflows to reach the peak in the fifth years, just to slow down afterwards for two years, to start a new recovery and so on.

As a general comment on the results of this scenario, we can say that the picture described is the one which most closely resembles the current behavior of the Mexican economy. Also important to note is the serious impact of the inflationary expectations on the general performance of the economy.

As an evaluation of the whole set, we can conclude, that the simulation results seem to suggest that the crude oil exports revenues are important enough to raise the level of economic activity. Also that the full play of government spending greatly improves the performance of the Mexican economy. Finally, that inflationary expectation have a very important impact on the behavior of the whole economy. The change in expectation turns the economy into a cyclical one with patterns of growth more consistent with the real facts.

"The Oil Revenues, Inflationary Expectations, and Domestic Monetary Policy": Scenario Set

This set contains scenario 7, which was named "Varying Oil Revenues Given Mild Inflationary Expectations and a Conservative Domestic Monetary Policy"; scenario 8 which was labeled "Varying Oil Revenues, Given Mild Inflationary Expectations and an Aggresive Monetary Policy"; and scenario 9 which is identified as "Varying Oil Revenues, Given Inflationary Expectations and Mild Domestic Monetary Policy."

The scenarios of this set are similar to those of the previous set, except that under this section a new policy variable is allowed to operate: The domestic monetary policy, meterialized by the changes in the amount of net domestic assets held by "El Banco de Mexico."

"Varying Oil Revenues Given Mild Inflationary Expectations and a Conservative Domestic Monetary Policy": Scenario (7)

Within this scenario, it is assumed that crude oil exports grow at a steady rate of 20 percent yearly, mild inflationary expectations[2] and that the domestic assets held by the central bank grow according to their growth rate.

According to the results of the simulation run, represented by the curves subindexed with the number seven, we can see that the inclusion of domestic monetary poli-

---

[2]Mild inflationary expectations according to the Mexican standards will be of the range of 20 to 24 percent annually.

109

cy helps to stabilize the economy which now grows in a
smooth cyclical fashion.

"Varying Oil Revenues Given Mild Inflationary Expectations and an Aggressive Monetary Policy": Scenario (8)

This scenario is similar to the previous one, except
that now, the amount of domestic assets held by the
central (the domestic component of the monetary base)
are allowed to grow at an ever increasing pace over the
period under consideration. The results out of the simu
lation run are represented graphically by the curves
subindexed with the number eight.

The results show the level of economic activity
until the forth period to be inferior to the levels reg-
istered in the previous scenario. By the fifth period
the level of real economic activity either measured by
real national income or real aggregate absorption sur-
passes those reported in the previous scenario just to
converge with them by the eigth period.

As an evaluation of the results coming out of this
scenario, we can say that the performance of the Mexican
economy is smoothly cyclical, being the cicles more pro-
nounced than in the previous scenario. Also the growth
of pattern is more uneven in this simulation run than
that shown by the Mexican economy in the previous
scenario.

"The Varying Oil Revenues Given Inflationary Expectations and Mild Domestic Monetary Policy":Scenario (9)

Within this scenario crude oil exports are allowed
to grow at a steady rate of twenty percent yearly. The
amount of not domestic assets held by the central bank
increase according to their rate of growth. High inflationary expectations are also assumed.

According with the graphical results represented by
the curves subindexed with the number nine, we have
that the overall performance of the economy is poorer
and more cyclical than in the two previous scenarios
already discussed. Again inflationary expectations seem
to be the leading force to distabilize the economy.
Instability, on the other hand, seems to lower the rate
of growth of the Mexican economy.

110

Conclusions

In general terms we can say that crude oil exports growing at a steady rate of 20 percent yearly are able to improve the overall performance of the economy, except in the case in which government spending is assumed away within a framework of inflationary expectations. This leads us also to conclude that currently the economic role of the government is very important as shown by the second and fourth simulation runs which present the economy stagnant and the economy booming, when government spending is excluded and when is introduced under non-inflationary circumstances, respectively.
We are also led to conclude that the growth of the domestic component of the monetary base which is expected to increase the money supply, in the short run run is able to improve the level of economic activity; finding which seem to lend support to the monetary view that the effect of monetary variables on real variables are short lived. Another conclusion is that the Mexican economy seems to possess a self corrective built in stability mechanism which might take to operate from three to four years to work out if allowed. Finally, there seems to be firm grounds to conclude that inflationary expectations are an important source of economic instability which slows down the level of economic activity, and prevents the economy from growing at rates compatibles with those under stable price expectations

FIGURE 3.1 Scenario Assumptions

SCENARIOS	GOVERNMENT SPENDING	CRUDE OIL EXPORTS	INFLATIONARY EXPECTATIONS	DOMESTIC COMP. OF MONET. BASE
1	INCORPORATED	20% YEARLY GROWTH	CONSTANT	CONSTANT
2	INCORPORATED	20% YEARLY GROWTH	MILD	CONSTANT
3	INCORPORATED	20% YEARLY GROWTH	HIGH	CONSTANT
4	NO	ONCE FOR ALL CHANGE	ONCE FOR ALL CHANGE	ONCE FOR ALL CHANGE
5	NO	20% YEARLY GROWTH	CONSTANT	CONSTANT
6	NO	20% YEARLY GROWTH	MILD	MILD GROWTH
7	INCORPORATED	20% YEARLY GROWTH	MILD	MILD GROWTH
8	INCORPORATED	20% YEARLY GROWTH	MILD	AGRESSIVE GROWTH
9	INCORPORATED	20% YEARLY GROWTH	HIGH	MILD GROWTH

The columns GOVERNMENT SPENDING, CRUDE OIL EXPORTS, INFLATIONARY EXPECTATIONS, and DOMESTIC COMP. OF MONET. BASE are grouped under the heading ASSUMPTION; the SCENARIOS / VARIABLES axis labels the rows.

4
Summary Report,
General Conclusions,
and Recommendations

SUMMARY REPORT

In Chapter 1 a brief historical perspective of the Mexican economy was outlined. Some economic interpretation of the historical facts is attempted in order to justify and lend support to the later inclusion of some variables in the econometric model which were expected to capture the essence of institutional considerations.

In Chapter 2 a sistematic development of the theory behind the econometric modelling is presented. Economic Theory and its mathematical specification are related hand by hand. This Chapter is the corner stone on which the econometric model is based upon.

Chapter 3 contains in its first section the empirical results stemming from the econometrics. In this chapter was presented an explanation and analysis of the results of the simulation model, under the different scenarios designed.

This chapter, which is very short, is a general assessment of the model and its results, as well as an evaluation of the shortcomings of the model. Some final comments are also made concerning data considerations.

Several apendices have been included. At the end of Chapter 3, Appendix A is included. It is a graphical presentation of the simulation results. Following the summary of results appendix B is presented. It is the presentation of the mathematical model which supports all the theoretical design of the econometric specifications.

GENERAL CONCLUSIONS

First of all, it may be stressed that the present
exercise, as far as it was carried, was attempted as a
scientific one. The theoretical choice was made on the
basis of how it was believed the chosen theory would be
able to describe and predict structural considerations
of the Mexican economy. Doctrinal considerations were
wholly unimportant.

As a general evaluation of this paper, we can say
that the economic specifications dealt with, based on
theory, institutional considerations and abstract reason
ing fit well with the Mexican data; also the econometric
exercise based on two stage least squares appeared to be
the correct one, to avoid the inconsistency implicit in
ordinary least squares, when dealing with simultaneous
equation systems as in the present system; and that the
econometric simulation model, fed with the econometric
results of the two stage squares exercise seems to re-
produce reasonably the behavior of the Mexican economy.

As a general assessment, it can be concluded that
growing out of our results there seems to be evidence
that a strategy of economic growth for the Mexican
economy based on carefully planned policy on oil price
exports and crude oil exports is possible as shown by
the simulation results. However, it must also be
stresssed that crude oil prices and crude oil exports
effects may be overcome or at least weakened by other
economic forces already present in the Mexican economy,
such as inflation which should be carefully assessed
and taken into consideration in the general growth
strategies. It is also important to emphasize that we
have carried the simulation experiment considering only
oil revenues arising out of crude oil exports, not because we believe this is the best alternative, but because this is the alternative so far exercised by the
Mexican government, and the most likely policy to be
followed in the time span under consideration. This
last consideration leads us to comment that a suitable
transformation of our model may allow us to consider and
to trace the implications of petrochemical development
by introducing some PEMEX blocks within the model. As
a general evaluation of the model, it can be said that
this relatively simple model is able to test an ample
variety of policies and allows the attainment of some
conclusions concerning the best alternative among the
policies considered.

On the limitations of the model, it should be noted
that the inclusion of some variables such as a short
term interest rate would have been highly desirable,
in the investment equations, and also as an argument for
the desired demand for money. However, the lack of

reliable data and the historical constraints imposed on
the behavior of the interest rate make it an empirical
burden on the modelling process rather than an empirical
support; also a finer breakdown of the model would have
been highly desirable for two reasons: first to reduce
the number of exogenous variables to deal with, and
second to allow a finer policy analysis. With regard to
the statistical base used to feed the model various
sources were consulted: several issues of the IMF financial statistics, different statistical reports produced by the office of statistics of El Banco de Mexico,
some data collection of the Secretaria de Programacion
y Presupuesto and some of the Wharton EFA. They were
sometimes difficult to reconcile, creating confusion and
uneasiness in the modelling process, especially during
the econometric estimations. To avoid major problems,
the statistics of the IMF and those of El Banco de Mexico were considered as the basic ones.

SUMMARY OF RESULTS
Aggregate Absorption

$$(1) \quad (\frac{GA}{P})_t = (\frac{C}{P})_t + (\frac{G}{P})_t + (\frac{PI}{P}) + (\frac{GI}{P})_t + (\frac{M}{PM})_t -$$

$$- (\frac{X}{PX})_t$$

Import prices

PM = PX

Real Private Consumption

$$(2) \quad (\frac{C}{P})_t = \begin{matrix}19.01\\(1.55)\end{matrix} + \begin{matrix}0.60\\(2.8)\end{matrix}(\frac{Y}{P})_t + \begin{matrix}0.5\\(0.53)\end{matrix}(\frac{MS}{P})_t -$$

$$\begin{matrix}123.9\\(-2.3)\end{matrix}\Pi^e_t$$

$$R^2 = 0.99 \qquad\qquad D.W. = 2.09$$

Real Government Expenditures

$$(3) \quad (\frac{G}{P})_t = \begin{matrix}-6.54\\(-2.99)\end{matrix} + \begin{matrix}0.149\\(3.45)\end{matrix}(\frac{MS}{P}) + \begin{matrix}0.072\\(4.2)\end{matrix}(\frac{Y}{P})_t +$$

$$\begin{matrix}66.9\\(2.99)\end{matrix}\Pi^e_t$$

$$R^2 = 0.97 \qquad\qquad D.W. = 2.03$$

$$(4) \quad (\frac{PI}{P})_t = \begin{matrix}-12.06\\(-0.72)\end{matrix} + \begin{matrix}0.32\\(1.42)\end{matrix}(\frac{Y}{P})_{t-1}\begin{matrix}-0.19\\(-2.55)\end{matrix}(\frac{Y}{P})_{t-2} -$$

$$\begin{matrix}-0.335\\(-0.65)\end{matrix}(\frac{MS}{P})_{t-1} + \begin{matrix}0.64\\(0.89)\end{matrix}(\frac{MS}{P})_{t-2} -$$

$$\begin{matrix}-0.045\\(-0.89)\end{matrix}\Pi^e_t$$

$$R^2 = 0.90 \qquad\qquad D.W. = 1.70$$

Real Government Investment

$$(5) \quad (\frac{GI}{P})_t = \begin{array}{c} -26.57 \\ (-4.61) \end{array} - \begin{array}{c} 0.34 \\ (-2.95) \end{array} (\frac{Y}{P})_{t-1} - \begin{array}{c} 0.138 \\ (-1.26) \end{array}$$

$$(\frac{Y}{P})_{t-2} + \begin{array}{c} 0.018 \\ (0.31) \end{array} (\frac{MS}{P})_{t-1} + \begin{array}{c} 1.785 \\ (2.97) \end{array} (\frac{MS}{P})_{t-2}$$

$$R^2 = 0.86 \qquad\qquad D.W. = 2.58$$

Real Imports

$$(6) \quad (\frac{M}{PM})_t = \begin{array}{c} 23.03 \\ (2.2) \end{array} - \begin{array}{c} 29.44 \\ (2.56) \end{array} (\frac{PM}{P})_t + \begin{array}{c} 0.93 \text{ E}-04 \\ (6.45) \end{array} (\frac{GA}{P})_t$$

$$R^2 = 0.92 \qquad\qquad D.W. = 1.69$$

Income and Excess of Capacity

$$(7) \quad (\frac{Y}{P})_t = (\frac{C}{P})_t + (\frac{G}{P})_t + (\frac{PI}{P})_t + (\frac{X}{PX})_t - (\frac{P}{PM})$$

Excess Capacity

$$(8) \quad (\frac{GAP}{P})_t = \begin{array}{c} 2898 \\ (1.39) \end{array} - \begin{array}{c} -0.278 \\ (-2.12) \end{array} (\frac{MS}{P}) + \begin{array}{c} 0.055 \\ (2.85) \end{array} Y^* +$$

$$\begin{array}{c} 0.71 \\ (3.03) \end{array} (\frac{GAP}{P})_{t-1}$$

$$R^2 = 0.84 \qquad\qquad D.W. = 2.06$$

General Price Level and Inflation

The Price Level

$$(9) \quad P_t = PT^{\theta 1} \ PM^{\theta 2}$$

Inflation

(10) $\quad \pi^d = \alpha_1 + \alpha_2 \ \ GAP + \alpha_3 \ \pi^e$

(11) $\pi = \begin{matrix} 0.049 \\ (1.9) \end{matrix} + \begin{matrix} 1.28 \\ (6.31) \end{matrix} \ \pi^e + \begin{matrix} 0.2 \\ (1.89) \end{matrix} \ \pi^i - \begin{matrix} 0.83E\text{-}05 \\ (-2.13) \end{matrix} \ (\frac{GAP}{P})$

$R^2 = 0.97 \quad\quad\quad\quad\quad\quad D.W. = 2.00$

$\pi^i = \dfrac{PM - PM_{t-1}}{PM_{t-1}}$

The Monetary Sector

The Money Supply

(12) $\quad MS = mH$

The Monetary Base

(13) $\quad H = NFA + NDA$

Net Foreign Assets Held by the Central Bank

(14) $\quad NFA = MBP + NFA_{t-1}$

(15) $\quad TT = \dfrac{PM}{P}$

The Monetary Multiplier

(16) $\quad m = \dfrac{\dfrac{C}{TD} + 1}{\dfrac{C}{TD} + R + \dfrac{XR}{TD}}$

Currency to Deposit Ratio

(17) $(\frac{C}{TD})_t = \underset{(2.4)}{0.5} - \underset{(-4)}{1.27} \Pi - \underset{(-0.3)}{0.0012}$ RUS $-$

$\underset{(-2.76)}{0.012}$ D1 $- \underset{(-4.09)}{0.019}$ D2 $- \underset{(7.09)}{0.026}$ D3 $+$

$\underset{(3.72)}{0.09}$ D38 $+ \underset{(5.43)}{0.12}$

$R^2 = 0.82$ D.W. $= 2.19$

The Short Term Interest Rate

(18) $R_{mex} = $ RUS $+$ IF

Institutional Factor

IF $= $ (D38 + D72) + (D65 + D68)

The Excess in Reserve to Total Deposits

(19) $(\frac{XR}{TD})_t = \underset{(0.35)}{0.02} + \underset{(0.42)}{0.00075} \Pi^e - \underset{(-0.29)}{0.005}$ RUS $+$

$\underset{(0.58)}{0.01}$ D65 $+ \underset{(0.68)}{0.034}$ D68 $+ \underset{(4.41)}{0.018}$ D1

$\underset{(-3.76)}{-0.015}$ D2 $- \underset{(-2.42)}{-0.015}$ D3 $+ \underset{(1.4)}{0.89} (\frac{XR}{TD})_{t-1}$

$R^2 = 0.89$ D.W. $= 2.07$

The Balance of Payments

(20) $MBP_t = $ TB + SCF + OIBR

(21) TB $= $ (X $-$ M)

$$(22) \quad SCF = \frac{57.29}{(2.96)} - \frac{1.79}{(-4.21)} dY_t - \frac{4.32}{(-1.5)} TB -$$

$$\frac{-44}{(2.84)} \quad RUS$$

$$R^2 = 0.8 \qquad\qquad D.W. = 2.8$$

(23) X = XOIL + NOILX

(24) XOIL = POIL * EXPOIL

(25) OIM = OILM * OIP

ENDOGENOUS VARIABLES

GA_t Nominal Aggregate Absorption

C_t Nominal Private Consumption

G_t Nominal Government Expenditures

PI   Nominal Private Investment

GI   Nominal Government Investment

M   Nominal Demand for Imports

P   General Price Level

Y   Nominal National Income

GAP   Difference between Normal or Permanent Income and Current National Income in Real Terms

Π^d Domestic Source of Inflation

Π Current Rate of Inflation

Ms   The Nominal Money Supply

H   The Monetary Base

NFA   Net Foreign Assets Held by the Central Bank

TT	Terms of Grade Between Mexico and the U.S.
m	The Money Multiplier
$(\frac{C}{TD})$	Currency to Total Deposits
R_{mex}	The Interest Rate
$(\frac{XR}{TD})_t$	Excess in Reserves to Total Deposits
MBP	Overall or Monetary Balance of Payments
TB	The Current Account Balance of Payments
SCF	Short Term Capital Flows
X	Nominal Exports
XOIL	Nominal Oil Exports
OIM	Nominal Oil Imports

EXOGENOUS VARIABLES

PM	Imports Price
PX	Exports Price
OILP	Price of Oil
Πe	Expected Rate of Inflation
Y^*	Permanent or Nomal Income
NDA	Net Domestic Assets
R	Legal Required Reserve
RUS	U.S. Short Term Interest Rate
D	Dummy Variable
$OIBP_t$	Residual Items in Balance of Payments
NOILX	Non-Oil Exports
EXPOIL	Oil Exports

Appendix A

The Simulation Results—
A Graphical Presentation

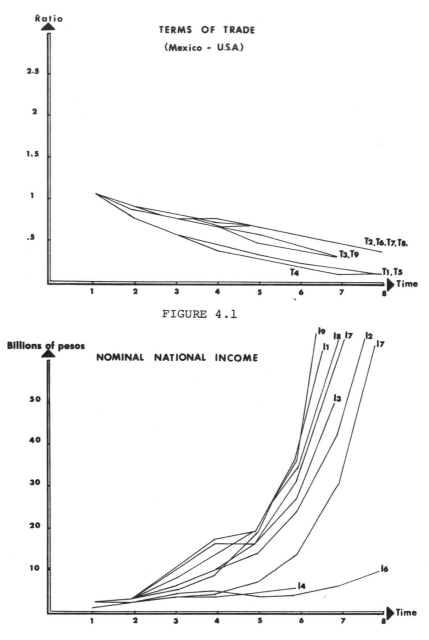

FIGURE 4.1

FIGURE 4.2

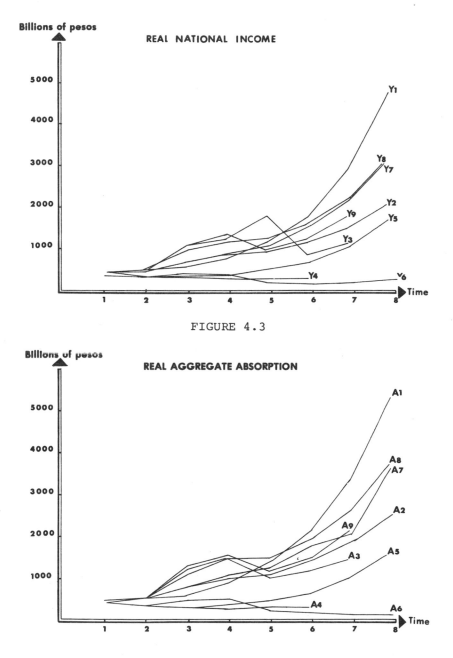

FIGURE 4.3

FIGURE 4.4

124

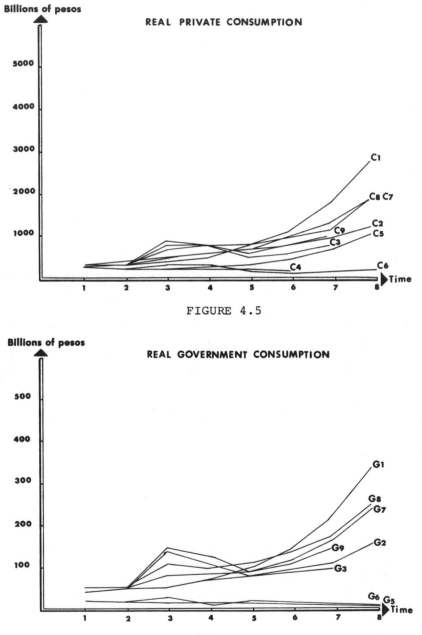

FIGURE 4.5

FIGURE 4.6

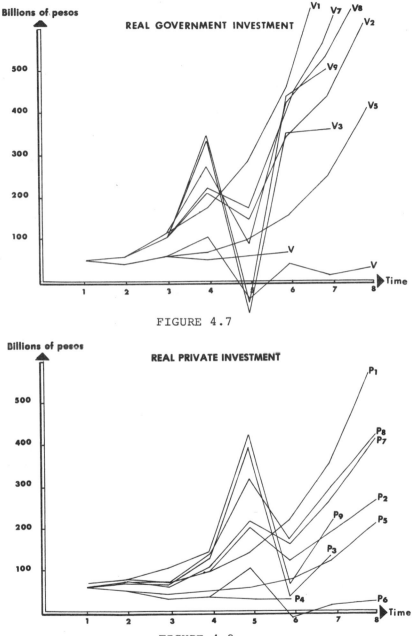

FIGURE 4.7

FIGURE 4.8

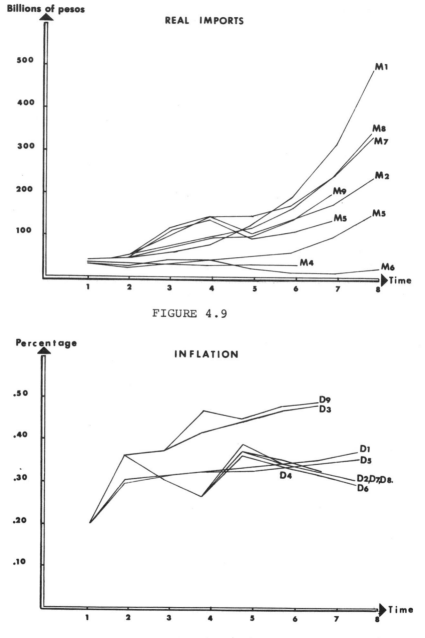

FIGURE 4.9

FIGURE 4.10

Appendix B

The Mathematical Model

MATHEMATICAL APPENDIX

The Oil Sector

(1) $TR = Rd - R_f$

(2) $Tc = Cd - C_f$

(3) $NR = TR - Tc - Tx$

Using (1) and (20 in (3) we have

(4) $NR = (Rd - Cd) \quad + \quad (R_f - C_f) - Tx$

Assuming that

(5) $Tx = nRd + mR_f - S$

(6) $Rd = PdQd$

(7) $R_f = PxQx$

(8) $Qd = Qd(y)$

(9) $Qx = Qx(Px, \frac{1}{y}\frac{dy}{df}, Rp)$

(10) $Rp = Rp(T, G)$

Using (5) through (10) in (4) we have

(11) $NR = [(1 - n) \; Pd \;\; Qd(Y) - Cd] +$

$\quad\quad\quad\quad + [(1 - m) \; Px \; Qx(Px, \frac{1}{y}\frac{dy}{df}, Rp(T, G)) - Cf] - S$

where

(12) $Cd = C_f$

List of Variables:

TR = Total PEMEX revenues

Tc = PEMEX's total cost

NR = Net PEMEX revenue after taxes

Rd = Domestic total sales

R_f = Foreign total revenue

Cd = Total PEMEX cost to produce oil goods sold
    domestically

C_f = Total PEMEX cost to produce exported crude
    oil

Tx = Total collected taxes

 n = Proposition of tax levied on domestic PEMEX
    sales

 m = Proposition of tax levied on foreign PEMEX
    crude oil products

 S = Government subsidies on domestic PEMEX sales

Pd = Weighted average domestic price of goods
    sold domestically by PEMEX

Px = Weighted average price on crude oil exports

Qd = Amount of oil product sold domestically

Qx = Amount of crude oil exports

 Y = Gross domestic product

R_p = PEMEX's proven reserves

 T = Technology

 G = PEMEX's expenditure on geological research

THE NON-OIL SECTOR
Real Income

In general equilibrum, we have

(1)   Ys = Yd

Substracting from both sides of (1) total sales of
PEMEX (the Mexican oil company), expressed in terms of
the Mexican currency (el peso) we have

(2) $(\frac{Y}{P})_t = (\frac{C}{P} + \frac{I}{P} + \frac{G}{P})_t + (\frac{X}{PX} - \frac{M}{PM})_t$

Using Alexander's approach, we can assume

$(\frac{GA}{P})_t = (\frac{C + I + G}{P})_t$

where the term on the left side is aggregate absorption. Using (2) in (1) and re-arranging the equation so that (GA/P) is on the right side, we have

(3) $(\frac{GA}{P})_t = \frac{Y}{P} + (\frac{M}{PM} - \frac{X}{PX})$

Since most of Mexico's international trade is with the United States, then it will be assumed that

(4)   PX = PM

Using (4) in (3) we have now

(5) $(\frac{GA}{P})_t = (\frac{Y}{P}) + (\frac{M - X}{PM})$

REAL AGGREGATE ABSORPTION

According to the theoretical framework used, real income is supposed to be equal to aggregate absorption, plus a flow demand for cash balances, that is,

(6) $(\frac{Y}{P})_t = (\frac{GA}{P}) + D_t$

hence,

$(\frac{D}{P})_t = (\frac{X - M}{PM})$

Bringing (GA/P) to the left side of (6) we have again

(7) $(\frac{GA}{P})_t = (\frac{Y}{P})_t - (\frac{D}{P})_t$

where the flow demand for money $(\frac{D}{P})_t$ is assumed to be dependent on the level of excess money supply and consumer's expectations formed according to the following scheme:

(8) $(\frac{D}{P})_t = \mu \ [\frac{M^*d}{P} - \frac{M_s}{P}]_t$; where

(8') $(\frac{D}{P})_t = d(\frac{M^*d}{P})_t$

THE STOCK DEMAND FOR MONEY

$(M*_d/P)_t$, the real stock demand for money, is supposed to be a fixed proportion of real income, that is,

(9) $(\dfrac{M*_d}{P}) = k(\dfrac{Y}{P})_t$

Substituting (9) in (8) and developing (8), we then have the flow demand for money:

(10) $(\dfrac{D}{P})_t = k\mu(\dfrac{Y}{P})_t - \mu(\dfrac{M_s}{P})_t$

Substituting (10) in (7), we transform the identity there into a behavioral equation as follows:

(11) $(\dfrac{GA}{P})_t = (1 - k\mu)\ (\dfrac{Y}{P})_t + (\dfrac{M_s}{P})_t$

PRIVATE CONSUMPTION

Private consumption is assumed to be a function of aggregate expenditures and expectations with regard the future rate of inflation, that is,

$(\dfrac{C}{P})* = P(\dfrac{GA}{P})_t + C_0\ \pi^e$

Using (11) in (12), we have

(13) $(\dfrac{C}{P})^d = P(1 - k\mu)\ (\dfrac{Y}{P}) + P\mu(\dfrac{M_s}{P})_t + C_0\ \pi^e$

It is also assumed that the dynamic pattern of consumption between periods is formed according to the following scheme:

(14) $d(\dfrac{C}{P})_t = q\ (\dfrac{C}{P})^*_t - (\dfrac{C}{P})_{t-1}$

Substituting (13 in (14), we have

(15) $(\dfrac{C}{P})_t = qP(1 - k\mu)\ (\dfrac{Y}{P}) + qP\mu(\dfrac{M_s}{P})_t + (1 - q)(\dfrac{C}{P})_{t-1} +$

$+ C_0\ \pi^e$

which is the behavioral equation for private consumption.

REAL GOVERNMENT EXPENDITURES

Desired government expenditures are also assumed to be a proportion "η" of aggregate expenditure plus some institutional factors, that is,

(16) $(\frac{G}{P})^* = \eta P(1 - k\mu)(\frac{Y}{P}) + \eta P\mu (\frac{M_s}{P})_t + g_1(IF)$

The dynamic adjustment of government expenditures and government expectations are formed according to the following scheme:

(17) $d(\frac{G}{P})_t = g\ (\frac{G}{P})^*_t - (\frac{G}{P})_{t-1}$

Using (16) in (17) we have now

(18) $(\frac{G}{P})_t = gP(1 - \mu k)(\frac{Y}{P})_t + gP\mu (\frac{M_s}{P})_t + (1 - g)(\frac{G}{P})_{t-1}$

$\qquad\qquad + g_1(\frac{IF}{P})_t$

Institutional factors could be measured by the current population level, since in Mexico an important role of government is to provide many of the basic social needs, such as roads, sewage, housing for the poor, hospital services and so forth, which usually grow in accordance with population. However, we decided not to include population as an explanatory variable for real government expenditures.

REAL PRIVATE INVESTMENT

Real private investment is assumed to depend upon the dynamic adjustment of the desired level of capital by entrepreneurs, that is,

(19) $(\frac{I}{P})_t = h^\lambda [K^d_t - K^d_{t-1}]$

where $\lambda = 0, 1$ and $0 < h < 1$; the desired level of capital stock is assumed to adjust according to the past performance of the economy measured by the leve of aggregate absorpiton, that is,

$$(20) \quad K_t^d = \alpha(\tfrac{GA}{P})_{t-1}$$

Substituting (20) into (19), we have

$$(21) \quad (\tfrac{I}{P})_t = \alpha h^0(\tfrac{GA}{P})_{t-1} - \alpha h^1(\tfrac{GA}{P})_{t-2}$$

Substituting (11) into (21), we have

$$(22) \quad (\tfrac{I}{P})_t = \alpha(1 - \mu k)(\tfrac{Y}{P})_{t-1} + \alpha\mu(\tfrac{M_s}{P})_{t-1} - \alpha h(1 - \mu k)(\tfrac{Y}{P})_{t-2} - \alpha h\mu(\tfrac{M_s}{P})_{t-2}$$

Re-arranging (22) we have the behavioral equation for real investment

$$(23) \quad (\tfrac{I}{P})_t = \alpha(1 - \mu k)(\tfrac{Y}{P})_{t-1} - \alpha h(1 - \mu k)(\tfrac{Y}{P})_{t-2} + \alpha\mu(\tfrac{M_s}{P})_{t-1} - \alpha h\mu(\tfrac{M_s}{P})_{t-2}$$

THE MONEY SUPPLY

We know that

$$(24) \quad M_{s_t} = CR_t + TD_t; \text{ and also that}$$

$$(25) \quad H_t = CR_t + R_t + XR_t, \text{ and additionally,}$$

$$(26) \quad R_t = \rho\, TD_t$$

Substituting (26) into (25), we have

$$(27) \quad H_t = CR_t + \rho\, TD_t + XR_t$$

Dividng (27) by TD_t we have

(28) $\dfrac{H_t}{TD} = (\dfrac{CR}{TD}) + \rho + (\dfrac{XR}{TD})_t$

THE CURRENCY TO DEPOSIT RATIO

It it is assumed that the ratio of currency to deposit depends on the opportunity cost of holding money, and the rate of inflation,

(29) $(\dfrac{CR}{TD})_t = \beta_0 + \beta_1 R_{mex} + \beta_2 \Pi_t + U,$

where R_{mex} (the opportunity cost of holding money), the short run domestic interest rate, is assumed to be equal to the world interest rate plus a risk factor to account for expected changes in the exchange rate and speculation, that is,

(30) $R_{mex} = RUS + RK$

where RK will be measured through a set of dummy variables.
Using (30) in (29), we have

(31) $(\dfrac{CR}{TD})_t = \beta_0 + \beta_1 RUS + \beta_1 RK + \beta_2 \Pi$

THE RATIO OF EXCESS RESERVES TO
TOTAL DEPOSIT

It is assumed that the desired excess in reserves $(\dfrac{XR}{TD})_t^*$ are a function of the opportunity cost of holding money and the expected rate of inflation, that is,

(32) $(\dfrac{XR}{TD})_t^* = \beta_3 + \beta_4 \Pi^e + \beta_5 R_{mex}$

Using (30) in (32) again, we have

(33) $(\dfrac{XR}{TD})_t^* = \beta_3 + \beta_4 \Pi^e + \beta_5 RUS + \beta_0 RK$

where the dynamic adjustment of the desired excess in reserves is assumed to be formed according to the following rational expectation model

(34) $d(\frac{XR}{TD})_t = x \ (\frac{XR}{TD})_t^* - (\frac{XR}{TD})_{t-1}$

Using (32) in (34), we have

(35) $(\frac{XR}{TD})_t = x\beta_3 + x\beta_4 \ \Pi^e + x\beta_5 \ RUS + x\beta_5 \ RK +$

$(1 - x) \ (\frac{XR}{TD})_{t-1}$

where we have the behavioral equation for the ratio of excess reserves to total deposits, where total deposits include demand plus time deposits. Substituting (31) and (35) into (28), we have

(36) $(\frac{H}{TD})_t = (\beta_0 + x\beta_3) + (\beta_1 + x\beta_5) \ RUS +$

$(\beta_1 + x\beta_5) \ RK + \rho + \beta_2 \ \Pi + x\beta_4 \ \Pi^e +$

$(1 - x) \ (\frac{XR}{TD})_{t-1}$

now if we divide (24) by (H_t), we have

(37) $(\frac{M_s}{H})_t = \frac{(CR)_t + (TD)_t}{H_t}$

If we divide the numerator and the denominator of the right side of (37) by $(TD)_t$, we have

(38) $(\frac{M_s}{H}) = \frac{(\frac{CR}{TD})_t + 1}{(\frac{H}{TD})_t}$

Finally, if we multiply (38) by H_t on both sides we have

(39) $M_{s_t} = [\frac{(\frac{CR}{TD}) + 1}{(\frac{CR}{TD}_t + \rho + (\frac{XR}{TD})_t}] \ H_t$

(40) $M_{s_t} = m \ H_t$

where the expression within parentheses is the money multiplier and H_t is the monetary base. The denominator in (39) is as expressed in (36) and M_{st} is the nominal supply of money.

THE MONETARY BASE

By definition, the monetary base has a domestic and a foreign component, that is,

$$(41) \quad H_t = NFA_t + NDA_t$$

THE OVERALL OR MONETARY BALANCE OF
PAYMENTS

By definition, the monetary balance of payments as overall result in balance of payments under fixed exchange rates is equivalent to the changes in net foreign assets and also equal to the total summation of its components, that is,

$$(42) \quad B_t = d\ NFA_t = (X + OILX)_t - (M - OILM)_t +$$

$$SCF_t + RIB_t$$

THE DEMAND FOR REAL IMPORTS

Real imports are assumed to be a function of the relative prices and the level of aggregate absorption, that is,

$$(43) \quad (\frac{M}{PM})_t = m_0 + m_1\ (\frac{PM}{P})_t + m_2 (\frac{GA}{P})_t$$

SHORT TERM CAPITAL FLOWS

The overall balance of payments is equal to the summation of capital and current account balances, that is,

$$(44) \quad B_t = d\ NFA_t = SCF_t + CAB_t + RIB_t$$

Bringing short term capital flows to the left side of (44), we have,

(45) $SCF_t = d\ NFA_t - CAB_t - RIB_t$

which is an identity. To transform it into a behavioral equation the following steps are taken: first if we recall from (9), the desired stock demand for nominal money is equal to

$$M*d = kY$$

and also from (40) and using (41) in (40) we know that the nominal stock of money supply is

$$Ms = m(NFA_t + NDA_t)$$

and assuming equilibrium in the stock money market we have

(46) $M*d = Ms$

Substituting (9) and (40 in (46) we have also that

(46') $Yt = \frac{m}{k}\ (NFA_t + NDA_t)$

differentiating (46') the equilibrium equation we have

(47) $\frac{dY}{dt} = \frac{m}{k} - \frac{d\ NFA}{dt} + \frac{m}{k}\ \frac{d\ NDA_t}{dt}$

Solving (47) by the net foreign assets held by the central bank

(48) $\frac{d\ NFA_t}{dt} = \frac{k}{m}\ \frac{dY}{dt} - \frac{d\ NDA_t}{dt}$

Substituting (48) into (45), we have

(49) $SCF_t = \frac{k}{m}\ dY_t - d\ NDA_t - CAB - RIB_t$

The short term capital flows (SCF) are assumed to be dependent also on institutional factors such as the changes in the opportunity cost of holding money, hence,

(50) $SCF = \frac{k}{m}\ dY_t - d\ NDA_t - CAB_t - RIB_t + \gamma\ d\ R_{mex}$

Using (30) in (50), we have

$$(51) \quad SCF = \frac{k}{m} \, dY_t - d \, NDA_t - CAB_t - RIB_t + \gamma \, dRUS +$$

$$+ \gamma \, dRK$$

THE PRICE INDEX

The price index is assumed to be the weighted average of tradable and non-tradable price indices, that is,

$$(52) \quad P_t = PT^{\theta 1} \, PH^{\theta 2}$$

where $\theta 1 + \theta 2 = 1$

THE INFLATION RATE

Transforming (52) in terms of rates of change, we have,

$$(53) \quad \frac{1}{P} \frac{dP}{dt} = \theta 1 \, \frac{1}{PM} \frac{dPM}{dt} + \theta 2 \, \frac{1}{PH} \frac{dPH}{dt}$$

THE DOMESTIC INFLATION

The rate of change of the price of non-tradable goods is assumed to depend on purely domestic variables, that is,

$$(54) \quad \frac{1}{PH} \frac{dPH}{dt} = W_0 + W_1 \, GAP + W_2 \, \Pi_t^e$$

Substituting (54) into (53), we have

$$(55) \quad \frac{1}{P} \frac{dP}{dt} = W_0 \theta 2 + \theta 1 \, \frac{1}{PM} \frac{dPM}{dt} + \theta 2 \, W_1 \, GAP + \theta 2 \, W_3 \, \Pi_t^e$$

In (55) we have expressed the rate of inflation as a function of the rate of imported inflation, the gap between normal and current income, and the expected rate of inflation.

THE GAP BETWEEN NORMAL AND CURRENT
INCOME

The dynamic adjustment of the gap between normal and current income is assumed to depend on flow demand for money and the excess of capacity available in the economy in the past period, that is,

$$(56) \quad d\ GAP_t = (\frac{D_t}{P})_t + \gamma G_{t-1}$$

Using (10) in (56), we have

$$(57) \quad d\ GAP_t = k\mu\frac{Y}{P} + \mu(\frac{M_s}{P}) + \gamma G_{t-1}$$

If we add and substract $(\mu k Y^*)$ on the right side of (57), we have

$$(58) \quad d\ GAP_t = \mu k(\frac{Y}{P}) + \mu k Y^* - \mu k Y^* + \mu(\frac{M_s}{P}) + \gamma\ G_{t-1}$$

Re-arranging (58), we have

$$(59) \quad GAP_t = -\mu k\ GAP_t + \mu k Y^* + \mu(\frac{M_s}{P})_t + (1+\gamma)\ G_{t-1}$$

Re-arranging (59), we get

$$(60) \quad GAP = -(\frac{\mu k}{1+\mu k})Y^* + (\frac{\mu}{1+\mu k})\frac{M_s}{P} + (\frac{L+r}{1+\mu k})\ G_{t-1}$$

THE EXPECTED INFLATION RATE

It is assumed that

$$(61) \quad d\ \Pi_t^e = \gamma[\Pi_{t-1} - \Pi_t^e - 1]$$

Developing Π_t^e from (61), we have

$$(62) \quad \Pi_t^e = \gamma\ \Pi_{t-1} + (1-\gamma)\ \Pi_{t-1}^e + \varepsilon_{1t}$$

To express Π_t^e in terms of Π_t variables, we proceed as follows: a) lag (61) one period and multiply the expression by $(1 - \gamma)$; then we have:

(63) $\quad (1 - \gamma) \, \Pi^e_{t-1} = \gamma(1 - \gamma) \quad \Pi_{t-2} + (1 - \gamma)^2 \, \Pi^e_{t-2} +$

$\quad + (1 - \gamma) \, \varepsilon_{t-1}$

Then, using (63) in (62), we get

(64) $\quad \Pi^e_t = \gamma \, \Pi_{t-1} + \qquad \gamma(1 - \gamma) \, \Pi_{t-2} + (1 - \gamma)^2$

$\qquad \Pi^e_{t-2} + \Omega_{1t}$

where $\Omega_{1t} = (1 - \gamma) \, \varepsilon_{1,t-1}$

or

(65) $\quad \Pi^e_t = \gamma \, \Pi_{t-1} + (1 - \gamma) \, \Pi_{t-2} + (1 - \gamma)^2 \, \Pi^e_{t-2}$

$\quad \Omega_{1t}$

and, in general:

(66) $\quad \Pi^e_t \quad = \gamma \, \Pi_{t-1} + \ldots + (1 + \gamma)^k \, \Pi^e_{t-k}$

It can bee seen in (66) that as the lag $\to \infty$, $(1 - \gamma) \to 0$; then for practical purposes we are expressing Π^e_t in terms of the observable variables Π_t

THE PERMANENT INCOME

With regard to y^*, it is assumed that

(67) $\quad Y^*_t - (1 + \iota) \, Y_{t-1} = \delta \, (\frac{Y}{P})_t - (1 + \iota) \, Y^*_{t-1}$

$\qquad + \varepsilon_{2t}$

Developing (67) and solving by y^*_t, we have

(68) $\quad y^*_t = \delta (\frac{Y}{P})_t + (1 + \iota) \, Y^*_{t-1} - \delta(1 + \iota) \, Y^*_{t-1}$

Re-arranging (68), we have

(69) $Y_t^* = \delta(\frac{Y}{P})_t + (1 - \delta)(1 + \iota) Y_{t-1}^* + \varepsilon_{2t}$

To express Y_t^* in terms of $(Y/P)_t$, we proceed as follows:
a) lag Y_t^* one period in (67) and then multiply it by
$(1 - \delta)(1 + \iota)$; thus, we have

(70) $(1 - \delta)(1 + \iota) Y_{t-1}^* = \delta(1 - \delta)(1 + \iota)(\frac{Y}{P})_{t-1} +$

$(1 - \delta)(1 + \iota)^2 Y_{t-2}^* + \varepsilon_{2,t-1}$

Substituting (70) into (60), we have

(71) $Y_t^* = \delta(\frac{Y}{P})_t + (1 - \delta)(1 + \iota)(\frac{Y}{P})_{t-1} +$

$(1 - \delta)(1 + \iota)^2 Y_{t-2}^* + (\varepsilon_{2t} + \varepsilon_{2t-1})$,

or

(72) $Y_t^* = \delta(\frac{Y}{P})_t + (1 - \delta)(1 + \iota)(\frac{Y}{P})_{t-1} +$

$(1 - \delta)(1 + \iota)^2 Y_{t-2}^* + \Omega_{3t}$

where $\Omega_{3t} = (\varepsilon_{2t} + \varepsilon_{2,t-1})$

It can be seen in (72) that as the lag $\rightarrow \infty$, $(1 - \mu)$
$(1 + \iota) \rightarrow 0$, thus for practical purposes, we are expressing Y_t^* in (72) in terms of the observable $(Y/P)_t$.

Index of Subjects

Agrarian Reform, 8

Aggregate, absorption, 62, 63, 64, 66, 85, 90, 91, 93, 102, 106; expenditures, 54, 57, 59, 67; income, 54; supply, 54, 57

Agricultural, development, 28, products of Mexico, 22, 23

Agriculture of Mexico, 18, 20

Asociacion Latinoamericana de Libre Comercio (ALALC), 36

Auto-Industry, 37

Banking industry, 38

Balance of payments, 49, 52, 53, 54, 68, 71, 72, 78, 84, 89, 102

Banco de Mexico, 40. See also Central Bank

Bank, Central, 8, 37, 68, 69, 71, 72, 78, 97; for economic development, 8. See also Nacional Financiera

Banking, Multiple, 38

Bond, Market, 91; price 91

Cambridge Cash Balance Approach, 60

Capital Flows, short

term, 12, 75, 78, 79, 84, 101

Consejo Nacional de Poblacion (CONAPO), 13

Confederation of Mexican workers, 14 (CTM)

Consumption, 54, 59, 62; government, 17, 40; desired private, 63; private, 17, 62, 63, 84, 85

Constitucion Mexicana, 4

Court, supreme, 3

Crude oil exports, 106, 113

Demand for money, 60 61, 77; for real cash balances, 60

Demographic explotion, 9

Devaluation, 26, 27

Development, urban, 10

Econometric, model, 102, 112; modelling, 112, 114; exercise, 113

Ejidatario, 20

Ejido, 20, 21

Encaje legal, 69

Entrepreneur, 65, 84, 90

Exchange rates, 73, 77, 78; fixed, 71

Fertility, the rate of, 9

Ferrocarriles Nacionales de Mexico, 29

Financial sector, 37

Flow demand, for money, 91,

142

Index of Names